CONTENTS

NYPD

LAUGHING IN THE LINE OF DUTY

BY

VIC FERRARI

INTRODUCTION

There are seventy-seven NYPD precincts spread out across New York City's five boroughs. From Riverdale to the Rockaways, every neighborhood has a police station with two green lanterns mounted above its doorway. You'd be hard-pressed to find an NYPD member who can explain the provenance of these gaudy light fixtures. Some say they are the gateways of law and order. Others believe they're antique bug zappers. No matter what they symbolize, NYPD police stations are open to the public twenty-four-seven. People visit their local precinct for many reasons. Some seek a form of justice. Others need an ear to bend. The unlucky get a guided tour of the building in handcuffs.

When you think about it, a precinct is a weighing station for society's ills. During my career with the New York City Police Department, I never realized that all of humanity funneled through the station house. There is no time for deep thought or reflection when you're on the inside looking out. NYPD cops live in the now, playing a twenty-year game of cat and mouse with their employer. You're a cog in a bureaucratic machine that views you as disposable. A hero one day, a goat the next; you can never train enough for a job that can kill you.

Most cops underestimate the enormity of their commitment after donning their shield for the first time. After a while, the shiny piece of tin resting above your heart becomes a part of you. You're young and naïve when you take the oath to protect and serve. Never in your wildest dreams could you imagine the situations you'll find yourself in or the people you'll meet.

1

You're about to learn about a subculture that most never experience. The world of law enforcement is secretive. We love to collect information, but we rarely share it with anyone outside the blue wall of silence. There's nothing dark or immoral. We're just a cautious group that likes to keep our affairs private. So please clear your mind of any preconceived notions about the NYPD because this book will be a real eye-opener.

To survive in law enforcement, you must be physically and mentally strong to deal with the long hours and less-than-hospitable working conditions. Police work is a young man's game where those under forty do the heavy lifting. Climbing fire escapes, foot chases, and standing in line for hours with a cranky prisoner at Bronx Central Booking are reserved for the young and idealistic.

You won't find an AARP member fighting crime in New York City. I recently saw a commercial where a sixty-something *Law & Order* actor races up a stairwell with a gun and kicks in a door. "When it gets intense on the set," he complains before segueing into the product he's pitching.

Intense? What does this schmuck know about making life-and-death decisions? When the director yells cut, he heads back to his air-conditioned trailer for his afternoon nap.

What goes on behind the scenes at the New York City Police Department is far more entertaining than anything you'll ever see on television. Sometimes, situations are so absurd that all you can do is laugh. This memoir is a collection of humorous and unbelievable stories from a twenty-year NYPD career.

Would you believe a dead man's unclaimed remains made daily stops to a kosher deli before an unconventional burial on a forgotten island?

Discover what happened after a mounted cop's horse dropped dead in the back of a Hell's Kitchen bar.

Did you know it's easier to steal a car with a pen than a screwdriver?

Learn why you should never trust an idiot with a bullhorn, and much more!

Those who have read my books know what to expect: a comical, introspective look into the NYPD. I pull back the curtain, exposing the hypocrisy and absurdity of the department. I pull no punches and let the horse chips fall where they may. So sit back and buckle up your seat belts because this is going to be a wild ride.

CHAPTER 1

QUEST FOR POWER

From the day I was born, I wanted to be a New York City police officer. Growing up, watching the cops chase the bad guys around the neighborhood resonated with me. As much as I aspired to become one of New York's finest, it never occurred to me to become a supervisor. When I entered the police academy, I wanted to learn as much as I could about investigating crime and catching criminals. Not managing my coworkers.

On my first day in the precinct, I noticed a great divide in the locker room. Most of my coworkers were hardworking men and women who put police work ahead of climbing the civil service ladder.

The only time you heard cops talking about becoming supervisors was six months before the sergeant's exam. Then, half the precinct had their faces buried in the patrol guide. Some cops wanted to rise through the ranks for better opportunities and a bump in pay. If you're stuck working midnights in a shitty precinct, the fastest way out is to pass the sergeant's exam. Then, you have those who have a quest for power.

They've been lying around the station house for years doing the bare minimum. One morning they wake up and want to play supervisor. These pinheads never worked a day in their lives and shouldn't be telling anyone what to do.

To become a sergeant, one must pass a civil service exam filled with obscure rules and regulations pulled from the bowels of the NYPD's patrol guide. The thick, outdated manual is twice the size of the Manhattan Yellow Pages. The NYPD sergeant's exam is riddled with absurd questions ranging from how to treat an injured horse to where they hide the toilet paper in the station house. Sadly, moving up in rank is based on memorization, not experience, character, or common sense. You could be the laziest piece of shit in the station house and take the sergeant's exam, provided you pay the filing fee.

And in the event that one of these clowns gets promoted, that's when the fun begins. Once they pin a sergeant's shield on their chest, everything changes. Now the job is on the level, and you had better take them seriously. But how can you? To see some clown who spent years tap dancing in the truancy unit show up in a busy precinct with sergeant stripes never sat right with me.

NYPD sergeants have tremendous responsibilities. Everything falls on them when something goes wrong. It was easy to tell who had street time when a group of newly promoted sergeants arrived at the precinct. The true believers followed the rules to the letter, while seasoned street cops could distinguish between the patrol guide and reality. A cop that's been around the block knows what to do when the shit hits the fan. In contrast, the former auxiliary coordinator manages like the captain of the *Titanic* when things go sideways. Streetwise probationary sergeants don't panic. They let the senior cops handle the sticky situations. The Kool-Aid drinkers doubled down and quoted the patrol guide, hoping it would part the Red Sea while leading them to the promised land.

When the faint of heart realized life as an NYPD supervisor wasn't what they had imagined, they'd seek refuge in clerical positions instead of putting in the street time needed to develop into effective supervisors.

Unfortunately, it's not always the best and brightest who rise through the ranks of the New York City Police Department.

NEVER TRUST AN IDIOT WITH A BULLHORN

A few weeks after graduating from the police academy, I got assigned to work the Easter Parade. As a naïve rookie cop, I didn't know what to expect for my first detail in Midtown Manhattan.

I was given a post along the parade route and told to stand up straight and face the crowd like a wooden Indian in a cigar store.

"It's not rocket science, kid. Just be visible and look professional," the old-time sergeant instructed.

The Easter Parade is an easy day for an NYPD patrolman. It's six hours of bonnets and bunnies handing out chocolates along Fifth Avenue. Unlike the West Indian or Puerto Rican Day Parades, there are no unruly drunks to deal with.

While enjoying the procession of colorful floats, I heard the piercing screech of a bullhorn.

"Face the crowd!" the amplified voice shouted.

"Who is that?" I asked the older cop standing beside me.

"Hennessey," he said.

"Who?" I repeated.

"Don't worry, kid, he'll introduce himself soon enough," the veteran cop replied, facing the crowd like a secret service agent.

There couldn't have been more than ten wide-eyed tourists on the other side of the wooden barrier when the bullhorn shrieked again, "I said to face the goddamn crowd!"

Whoever was screaming into that thing was getting closer. I felt like a child told to stand in the corner while debating turning around. The bullhorn was in charge. I learned that lesson the hard way eight years earlier from the nuns at Monsignor Scanlan High School. Challenging the bullhorn brought consequences.

As I struggled with my decision, I reflected on my Catholic upbringing. God warned Adam and Eve not to eat the apple. Lot's wife had to have that last look before she turned to salt. It's human nature to question authority. And despite the consequences, I had to see who the lunatic with the bullhorn was.

When I turned to survey Fifth Avenue, I locked eyes with a short, middle-aged lieutenant in a ceremonial summer blouse who came charging at me like an aggressive peacock.

"What have I been saying all day long? Face the goddamn crowd," he barked in a thick Irish brogue.

"Sorry, Lieutenant," I replied.

"Ferrari, if there's a sniper in the crowd, you'd never see him!" he shouted inches from my face.

Sniper? Who the hell wants to kill the Easter Bunny?

The peacock put down his bullhorn long enough to write my name and shield in his little black book before running full speed into a crowd of parasols and Victorian hats.

Humiliated in front of the parade route, I tried to pull myself together when the older cop came over to console me.

"I see you've met Lieutenant Hennessey," he laughed.

"What just happened?" I asked.

"You just got a command discipline," the cop replied, patting me on the shoulder.

"For what?" I said.

"Don't take it personal, kid. Hennessey hates everyone," he explained.

That wouldn't be the last time I had to deal with the little peacock who ruled the borough of Manhattan South with an iron fist.

The NYPD divides the densely populated borough of Manhattan in two. Patrol Borough Manhattan North covers 59th Street to the Bronx border. Patrol Borough Manhattan South runs south of 59th Street to the Staten Island Ferry. There are many perks for cops working south of Spanish Harlem. Better food, less crime, and the chance to rub elbows with New York City's rich and famous. Making contacts with Manhattan powerbrokers can lead to lucrative second careers.

Most Midtown cops don't want to rock the boat and risk getting kicked out of their cushy precincts. One Police Plaza is well aware of this and stocks its patrol boroughs covering the coveted precincts with henchmen like Hennessey to keep everyone in line.

The peacock relished his assignment and tormenting cops with his bullhorn. Hennessey preferred the ceremonial summer blouse or heavy wool reefer coat during the winter months over the standard NYPD duty jacket so he would stand out in a crowd. Both outer garments look sharp but are impractical for police work because they restrict your movement. The reefer coat feels like a rented tuxedo you can't wait to return after a wedding.

Hennessey looked more like the master of ceremonies at a communion breakfast than a borough lieutenant. He never broke character, maintaining the tough guy act at all times. I'm sure he patterned his persona after the hard-nosed Captain McCluskey in *The Godfather*. Unlike the towering Sterling Hayden, Hennessey was a pipsqueak whose power came from his pen.

Hennessey wielded tremendous power for a lieutenant. He was free to micromanage every parade, demonstration, and union strike as he saw fit.

Whenever I got stuck working a uniformed detail in Lower Manhattan, I'd do my best to stay out of his way. But that was easier said than done. Hennessey had the energy of a five-year-old and would fly around like a pesky mosquito looking to bite anyone he could get his hands on.

Later in my career, Hennessey caught me and several coworkers chatting along the parade route of the Saint Patrick's Day Parade. Before we could take off, he came rushing over. "What is this? A fucking PBA (Patrolmen's Benevolent Association) meeting?" he shouted.

No longer intimidated, I smiled as Hennessey copied my name and shield number again in his little black book.

"Laugh, Ferrari, but every one of you would be dead if someone tossed a grenade into this group," he lectured.

Grenade? We're standing in front of FAO Schwarz. Would someone tell this guy to lighten up?

"Well, gents, you're all off-post. I'm going to have to stick one in your asses," the old son of a bitch mocked before dashing into the crowd of bagpipes and kilts.

Hennessey spoke with the grace of an Irish poet and supervised like Idi Amin. He was famous for his sarcastic sonnets when handing out a command discipline.

"I traveled three thousand miles to be your boss, and your boss I'll be," he'd lecture in his heavy Irish accent. You couldn't get through a parade without the little prick letting you know who was in charge.

Hennessey didn't have many friends in the department, and that was fine with him. God had put him on this earth to ensure anyone below the rank of lieutenant wouldn't get a moment's peace when he was around.

A week after the St. Patrick's Day Parade incident, my lieutenant called me into his office.

"Hey, Vic, I see you got a command discipline from Patrol Borough Manhattan South," he said.

"Yeah, Lou (lieutenant)," I grumbled.

"Hennessey?" my lieutenant laughed.

"You know him?" I asked.

"I went through the police academy with him in 1965."

"What was he like back then?" I asked.

"Hennessey was an asshole then, and he'll be an asshole till the day he dies," my lieutenant replied, tearing up the command discipline into little pieces.

"Thanks, Lieutenant," I said, turning to leave the room.

"Hey, Vic, don't forget, the man traveled three thousand miles to be your boss," he laughed before tossing the scraps of paper into the wastebasket.

YOU REMEMBER JOHNNY JONES?

My first command was a burned-out precinct in the South Bronx. The NYPD dumping ground known as Hotel California was a weighing station for grizzled middle-aged drunks and Vietnam vets biding their time until retirement.

It was a tough place to work for a young cop looking to make a difference. "Figure it out, Rookie," the salty old-timers mocked when you asked a question. As nasty as the old timers could be, it was the two-year veterans that treated the rookies worse.

One guy I avoided like a bad case of the crabs was a big-mouthed rookie wrangler with questionable motives. At twenty-five years old, he lumbered around the precinct like he owned the place, barking orders at inexperienced cops who wouldn't tell him to fuck off.

Rookie cops are eager-to-please puppies who follow the loudest voice in the locker room. And no voice was louder than Lard-ass Larry, a vile individual who took full advantage of the rookies' naivete.

He treated every incoming class of rookie cops as a concierge service. Fetching his lunch or cleaning his guns was the price of acceptance. Lard-ass Larry was infamous for pawning off bullshit arrests on young and impressionable cops who didn't know any better.

"Here you go, kid," the cocksure twenty-five-year-old would say while handing them a sack of shit.

After a while, you realize the schmuck you've been following wasn't acting in your best interests. Once that light goes on, you distance yourself from the guy hustling you for drinks at the bar.

When he wasn't bamboozling rookies, the fat bastard was sleeping on the lunchroom couch. It didn't take me long to realize that Lard-ass Larry was a lazy scumbag, and it was time to check out of Hotel California. I transferred from the downtrodden precinct to the cushy Riverdale section of the Bronx. I lost track of Lard-ass Larry for several years until I ran into him in the precinct stairwell.

The third floor of the precinct housed the narcotics division, where disheveled undercover detectives would slide through the rear entrance of the building before disappearing into an elevator.

One afternoon, I bumped into a dumpy red-faced cop lugging a battering ram up the stairwell.

"Hey, Ferrari, long time no see," he said.

"Larry, how are you? You know we have an elevator," I mocked, pointing to the battering ram.

"I figured I'd get a little exercise," he laughed.

"I see you decided to join the working class," I said.

"Yeah, can't work in the precinct forever," he smugly replied as the sweat rolled down his chubby face.

"Work?" This guy never worked a day in his life.

Having worked in the narcotics division, I found it ironic to see someone as lazy and out of shape as a Lard-ass Larry carrying a battering ram. The narcotics division is fast-paced, requiring lots of stamina. I was involved in weekly foot chases, not to mention wrestling with suspects trying to flush evidence down the toilet. Lard-ass Larry stood out like a sore thumb in the narcotics division.

Ten seconds after our impromptu reunion, I was on the phone with a friend who worked with him.

"Lard-ass Larry is in the narcotics division?" I asked.

"Yeah, he's useless," my friend laughed.

"What do they use him for?" I asked.

"Not much. The fat bastard has only been here a month and is already trying to slide into an administrative position," my friend replied.

I wasn't surprised. Guys like Lard-ass Larry are in over their heads when it's time to take out the handcuffs. After a while, your coworkers notice who's the last one through the door on a search warrant. Larry's physical limitations and reluctance to work sparked animosity among his coworkers. I felt for my friend, who got saddled with a lazy loudmouth that somehow weaseled his way into the narcotics division.

It would be another ten years before I saw Lard-ass Larry again. This time he ambushed me in the arrest-processing room of a Bronx precinct.

"Detective Ferrari. You got a second?" a voice called over my shoulder.

When I turned, I was greeted by a fat middle-aged man in a cheap suit blocking the doorway. *Where do I know this guy from?* I pondered, trying to place a name with the face when it hit me.

"Hey, Larry," I replied, continuing to fill out my paperwork.

Whoever sold him that polyester suit had a great sense of humor and was laughing all the way to the bank with their five-dollar commission. As amusing as the suit was, the gold sergeant's shield pinned to his waist got my attention.

"I need to see you in my office," he ordered before turning around and walking out of the room.

This guy is a sergeant running a precinct detective squad? I must be dreaming.

I remembered this clown unconscious in the precinct lounge while it was all hands on deck on busy summer nights. Somehow this lazy sack of shit passed a sergeant's exam and convinced someone downtown he was a savvy gumshoe capable of heading investigations.

There were no pleasantries or friendly handshakes. Whatever was on this douchebag's mind was business. And by the looks of things, I would be on the business end. After leading me into his office, he told me to close the door as he maneuvered his wide ass around a desk before dumping it in a swivel chair. He dug through a drawer before producing a photograph.

"You remember Johnny Jones?" he asked, shoving the picture in my face.

"Of course, Larry," I replied, glancing at the photo.

Johnny Jones was a man you didn't want to cross. The hulking army ranger did several tours in Vietnam before becoming a member of New York's finest. Johnny kept to himself, riding around the precinct in his scooter before the crack of dawn. When he wasn't handing out parking tickets, he was in the precinct gym pumping iron.

Tall and muscular with a thousand-yard stare, Johnny Jones was not someone to provoke. In my short time in the precinct, I had seen firsthand how unpredictable he could be.

Once at a precinct club meeting, he accused another cop of cheating during a friendly poker game. When the cop laughed off the accusation, Johnny pulled him from his chair like a ragdoll and slammed his head into the jukebox, knocking him unconscious.

I worked with the volatile Vietnam veteran once, and it left a lasting impression. Unlike most of the burned-out old-timers, Johnny was cordial. He said little for the first half of our tour before opening up about his days as a door gunner raking the Vietnam countryside with machine gunfire.

As an impressionable rookie cop, I listened, careful not to interrupt the stoic warrior as he bared his soul to the horrors of war. As interesting as his stories were—mowing snipers out of trees with an M60 machine gun—he shared another story that made me realize he was not to be toyed with.

After working a midnight shift, Johnny Jones went home to his University Heights apartment to catch some sleep. After dozing off, he was awakened by someone picking his door lock.

"Jesus, Johnny. What did you do?" I asked.

"I pulled open the door and dragged that motherfucker inside my apartment," he replied.

"I'll bet the cops that responded found that pretty funny," I said.

"Cops? I didn't call the cops. I beat the daylights out of him before tossing him back into the hallway," Johnny explained.

I couldn't imagine what it would be like to be in a bare-knuckle brawl with a man of Johnny Jones's size. In all probability, the hapless burglar was beaten to a pulp.

I knew to keep my mouth shut. Throughout the conversation, I smiled and nodded while telling myself I had better not piss this guy off. I never gave Johnny Jones a second thought until eighteen years later, when Lard-ass Larry was waving his photo in my face.

"We're looking for him," he replied, studying my face.

"What did he do?" I asked.

"His wife filed a domestic violence complaint against him," Lard-ass Larry replied.

"Okay," I said, handing back the photo.

There are detectives, and there are guys who pretend to be detectives after watching too many episodes of *Law & Order*. Lard-ass Larry fell into the latter category as he adjusted his tie, getting ready to hit me with the next question.

Channeling his best Keith Morrison imitation, he asked, "What kind of guy would you say Johnny Jones is?"

What an odd question to ask. My only connection to Johnny Jones was that we worked in the same precinct almost two decades ago. We weren't friends or steady partners. Lard-ass Larry knew this because he began his career in the same precinct before I arrived and remained long after I had left.

For the life of me, I couldn't figure out what I was doing in this jerkoff's office. Then it hit me.

The chickenshit didn't want to explain to his detectives how unpredictable the Vietnam veteran could be. If he did, he'd be expected to be out there searching for his former coworker. Instead, he wanted to use me as a source to distance himself in case the apprehension went wrong.

"Larry, are you kidding me?" I asked.

"No, Vic, I'm not," Sergeant Fat-ass replied.

"Larry, I was in the precinct for less than a year. I didn't know the guy."

For twenty years, Lard-ass Larry pretended to be a cop without having to get his hands dirty. Now tasked with a volatile situation, he wanted to use me to avoid sticking his neck out. I saw through his ruse and played dumb.

"Larry, you know more about the guy than I would. Didn't you work in the precinct for seven years?" I replied, before excusing myself.

The problem with guys like Lard-ass Larry is that after years of passing the buck they don't know what to do when their feet are held to the fire. Johnny Jones was his problem, not mine. I'm sure Lard-ass Larry had many sleepless nights while his detectives searched for the loose cannon. If he had been upfront and honest about what he was looking for, I would have offered my opinion, which would have been the same as his.

SUPER MARIO

I learned many lessons during my law enforcement career. The one that stands out is the New York City Police Department doesn't trust its employees. No agency in the world seconded-guesses its staff more than the NYPD. It's not like you walked in off the street, were handed an apron, and told to make a vanilla latte. Before entering the NYPD police academy, recruits undergo physical and psychological exams, drug screening, and a rigorous background check. After investing all that time and money, you would think the department would feel secure with the people they hire to protect and serve.

The reality is they don't. The NYPD has countless rules and regulations to keep its members in line. Most supervisors understand this and ignore the picayune crap. Then, you have those who believe everything they've read between the pages of the patrol guide. They go by the book while the world comes to a grinding halt.

Not everything is black and white in law enforcement. There's a large gray area governed by compassion and common sense. The supervisors who understand this are respected by their subordinates. The ones who don't will fight you tooth and nail over the department's ridiculous mandates.

You'll run into these jackasses when passing through hostile territories like Queens or Manhattan South. They don't trust their subordinates, and they certainly don't trust anyone who drops in for the day.

This can be a pain in the ass when you're assigned to a citywide unit like the Auto Crime Division. Bouncing around the different boroughs, you're not always current with new directives or policy changes until one smacks you in the face.

I'd often get into hot water after ignoring some ridiculous edict that kept me from doing my job. One such rule change arose after an arrest I made in Manhattan. On the surface, it was an open-and-shut case. After running the plate of a stolen Honda Accord, my partner and I arrested the driver and impounded the vehicle.

The fly in the ointment was the vehicle's owner was moving out of the country the following week. Based on my conversation with the victim, the district attorney could write the complaint. But if the case went to the grand jury, the victim would have to testify or provide an affidavit for the case to move forward.

To ensure the case got handled properly, I arranged to meet the complainant at the Manhattan courthouse.

As I was about to leave the precinct, my partner said: "You know you're supposed to write this up online."

In the early nineties, the NYPD developed the video booking program to reduce arrest overtime. Instead of cops traveling to the courthouse to meet with a district attorney to file charges, it was done by teleconference. Theoretically, the program would save time and money by reducing travel time. However, things didn't always go as planned. Poor internet connections and jammed fax machines often caused cases to get bungled or tossed out.

"What am I supposed to do? Let the case fall apart because they don't want to pay for an hour of overtime?" I replied.

"I'm just telling you, they might break your balls if you show up to the courthouse," my partner laughed.

I ignored the ridiculous mandate and drove to the Manhattan district attorney's office. While waiting for my victim to arrive, I decided to grab a snack from a vending machine.

While digging through my pocket for change, I noticed a young court officer in his bright, shiny uniform giving me the hairy eyebrow.

"Go ahead. I haven't decided what I want," I said, stepping away from the machine.

"What do you think you're doing?" he growled.

"I'm trying to figure out what I want for dinner," I replied.

What's this guy's problem?

Court officers are responsible for the security of the courthouse. Normally, they have a great working relationship with the NYPD. I wasn't in an unauthorized area and had my detective shield hanging on a lanyard around my neck. This guy was taking his job a bit too seriously.

"What's your command?" he barked.

"Listen, Junior, why don't you run along?" I said, dropping coins into the vending machine.

"What did you just say?" he yelled as he unzipped his navy-blue jacket, revealing an NYPD sergeant's shield pinned to his white shirt.

Now everything made sense. The young sergeant appeared to be a court officer without his sergeant's shield exposed. Most sergeants working inside details wear the navy-blue NYPD uniform shirt. This pinhead was wearing his white ceremonial shirt and looked like a court officer.

It was a simple case of mistaken identity, but the junior sergeant wasn't letting it go. He pulled a notepad from inside his jacket and started drilling me with questions.

I felt like a prisoner of war, providing name, rank, and serial number while he began writing me up for a command discipline.

I was screwed. You can't mouth off to a supervisor and not expect repercussions. If I was lucky, I'd get a command discipline for not adhering to the video booking rule. If he wanted to be a real hard-ass, he could try to bring me up on insubordination charges that would carry a much stiffer penalty.

"Come with me," he said, leading me to an office at the back of the courthouse.

I had to think of something fast before the rookie sergeant began making phone calls and causing me all kinds of trouble.

"Hey, Vic, long time no see!" a familiar voice shouted from the back of the room.

Justin Flynn and I met in grammar school. As teenagers, we worked together at McDonald's, and I once dated his older sister. Flynn was a great guy, but more importantly, he was an NYPD lieutenant assigned to the Manhattan court system.

"Justin, how the hell are you?" I said, walking past the surprised young court officer/sergeant.

"What brings you down here?" he replied, grabbing me in a bear hug.

"Funny you should ask," I laughed.

"Vic, have a seat. You want coffee?" my high school buddy asked.

"Nah, I'm good," I said, plopping down in a chair beside his desk.

Still holding onto his notepad, the young sergeant looked to the floor. An uncomfortable silence fell upon the small room, prompting Flynn to ask, "What's going on?"

"Lieutenant, this detective was disrespectful and insubordinate," the sergeant said.

"What happened, Vic?" Flynn asked.

"Justin, he ambushed me in the hallway, asking all sorts of questions. I thought he was a court officer and told him to get lost," I replied.

"Mario, I'd like you to meet an old friend of mine, Vic Ferrari," Flynn said.

Still trying to push the issue, the young sergeant asked, "Lieutenant, may I have a word with you?"

I took the hint and stepped outside the office while Flynn calmed the young sergeant down. I wasn't too worried. I knew my old friend wouldn't let this douchebag write me up over a case of mistaken identity.

A few minutes later, I got called back into the room.

"Okay, guys, this was a big misunderstanding. I'd like you two to shake hands and put this behind you," Flynn said.

I shook the sergeant's limp hand while he gritted his teeth before quickly leaving the room.

"Pleasant guy," I mocked.

"He's one of these guys who should have learned to be a cop before taking the sergeant's exam," Flynn replied.

"I'll never understand a guy like that," I said.

"Well, look where he is now. He spends less than six months as a sergeant in a precinct before transferring to the court section,"

"Let me guess, he's already studying for the lieutenant's exam?" I asked.

"He has his head buried in that fucking patrol guide eight hours a day. I'm surprised he had the time to fuck with you," Flynn laughed.

I thanked my childhood friend for getting me out of a sticky situation before finishing up with my arrest. I had many a dust-up throughout my NYPD career with guys like Super Mario. The odds of running into him again were slim, provided I stayed away from the Manhattan court section during the four to twelve shift. But that was easier said than done.

A few years later, I was contacted by an investigator from the New York State Department of Motor Vehicles. He had a case with a late-model Toyota Highlander in the Bronx that was registered with fraudulent documents. Instead of trekking down from Albany to inspect the potentially stolen vehicle, the investigator asked if I could look into it for him. On the surface, it was a gift that had fallen into my lap. If the vehicle was stolen, I would have an easy arrest. When finished, I'd send the paperwork to Albany, where the DMV investigator would close out his case.

Before looking for the vehicle, my partner and I decided to grab a bite to eat. While searching for a parking spot near a neighborhood deli, I spotted the Toyota Highlander double-parked on Eastchester Road.

"Holy shit, what kind of luck is that?" my partner said as we pulled behind the sleek black SUV.

We exited our vehicle and approached the double-parked SUV.

"Police. Can you please roll down your window?" I asked, gently tapping on the driver side window with my finger.

The driver smiled before rolling down his window and asked, "What's the problem?"

"You're double parked. Can I please see your license and registration?" I asked while examining the vehicle's vehicle identification number (VIN) on the dashboard.

"No problem," he replied.

The vehicle identification number was forged and looked like something from a third-grade art class. That was bad news for the driver, who didn't seem to have a care in the world. He kept smiling and cracking jokes while rummaging around the vehicle's interior for his paperwork.

After several minutes, the driver slowly slid his license, registration, and NYPD police identification card through the open window.

"I'm on the job," the young cop said with a smile.

I felt a knot in my stomach. This wouldn't be a simple arrest for a stolen vehicle. My gift from Albany had turned into a nightmare. I couldn't let the young cop drive off with the stolen vehicle, and I couldn't arrest him without a supervisor present.

"Where do you guys work?" the young cop asked.

"Auto Crime Division," I replied.

"Is there a problem with my vehicle?" he asked.

Problem? There was a problem, all right.

Whether he knew it or not, the young cop's career was on hold for the unseen future. The wheels of justice move slowly for NYPD members accused of impropriety. You can languish for years without your gun and shield, working midnights in some hellhole before you're cleared of an allegation.

"I'm not sure. But I need you to follow me to the precinct," I said.

The young cop complied as my partner and I returned to our vehicle.

"What now?" my partner asked.

"I'm calling Frank (our sergeant)," I replied.

I started kicking myself in the ass for getting involved with this investigation as I dialed my office. I was in a no-win situation. If I squashed the case, I'd lose my job. If the cop got suspended or fired, I'd be branded a rat. You try to do the right thing when dealing with off-duty cops, but this was way out of bounds.

NYPD members tend to look the other way when dealing with their own when it comes to minor infractions. But this wasn't tearing up a parking ticket for an off-duty cop. It was a criminal investigation of a member of the service (MOS), and I had to deal with it.

"Hey, Frank. I have a situation here," I said into the phone.

"What's up, Vic?" my sergeant asked.

Frank Triola was the consummate professional. He trusted his detectives and gave them a lot of leeway. Above all, Frank knew how to deal with volatile situations. When the shit hit the fan, Frank was cool as a cucumber.

"Frank, I'm heading into the Forty-Ninth Precinct with an MOS with a stolen vehicle," I said.

"What's he saying about the vehicle?" my sergeant asked.

"Not much, but I'd appreciate it if you could come here as soon as possible," I said.

"No problem, Vic. Sit tight, and I'll be there shortly. You know I have to tell Chumley and notify IAB (Internal Affairs Bureau)."

I knew IAB was coming to the party. That went without saying. Those scumbags would run out of the building to catch a cop leaving work ten minutes early and would jump at the opportunity for something like this.

When we arrived at the precinct, my partner brought the off-duty cop up to the detective squad while I inspected the Toyota Highlander.

Whoever changed the vehicle identification number on the dashboard had done a sloppy job. I had to crawl beneath the vehicle with a flashlight to read the confidential vehicle identification number stamped on the frame. After obtaining the true VIN, I learned the vehicle had been stolen from a car dealership in Orlando a month earlier.

When I went inside the precinct to wash up, I was greeted by my sergeant, who had already interviewed the off-duty cop.

"What's his story?" I asked.

"He said he purchased the truck two weeks ago from a mechanic on Jerome Avenue," my sergeant said.

"How much did he pay for it?"

"Thirty-five thousand dollars."

"Let me guess, he paid cash, doesn't have a receipt," I asked.

"Yup," my sergeant laughed.

I had heard this story many times before.

In cases like this, the buyer knows they've purchased a stolen vehicle for below the market price. If caught, they give a vague explanation of a mysterious mechanic or car salesman who duped them. The story unwinds when you ask them to show a paper trail for the money used to purchase the vehicle.

Things were not looking good for the off-duty cop. Possessing a stolen vehicle would be the end of his NYPD career.

"Orlando, Florida. That's a long way for a stolen vehicle to travel," I said.

"What are you thinking?" my sergeant asked.

"I think there's an organized ring transporting stolen vehicles up the East Coast."

While my sergeant and I discussed the off-duty cop's culpability, the Bronx duty captain arrived with two clowns dressed like they worked at the Gap. Khakis and docksides might play well on Netflix cop shows, but they're not practical for police work. The only place where Connecticut casual is worn is the Internal Affairs Bureau.

"The rat patrol is here," my sergeant whispered.

The duty captain was cordial, thanking my sergeant and me for following NYPD protocol.

"Things like this can't be swept under the rug," the old-time captain said.

As the captain rambled on about the dangers of police corruption, I could feel one of the Gap employees giving me a dirty look. When I turned my head, I muttered, "Ah shit."

Super Mario was back. This time as a lieutenant in the Internal Affairs Bureau. Less than two years after our courthouse dust-up, the skinny weasel had passed another civil service exam. I wasn't looking forward to working with IAB. Now, I had to deal with someone who already had a hard-on for me.

The duty captain picked up on the hard stare and asked, "I'm guessing you two don't socialize."

"Something like that," I replied.

"All right, let's put all that shit behind us and get to work," the captain said.

I was interviewed under oath, meaning I had to explain in great detail how everything went down. I felt like I was testifying before Congress, speaking into a microphone while the supervisors watched my every move. I had done everything by the book. But it sure felt like I was in the hot seat.

Unfortunately for me, Super Mario was heading the investigation. I explained to him and his flunky that the off-duty cop's phone and bank records were key to the investigation.

"Why would we need that?" Super Mario asked.

"You have to follow the money," I explained.

"What money?" Super Mario asked.

"The thirty-five thousand dollars he claims he paid for the vehicle," I replied.

I provided Super Mario with a contact number for the Department of Motor Vehicle investigator and all the pertinent paperwork.

If Super Mario were smart, he'd follow my blueprint to sort out this mystery. After three hours of speaking into a tape recorder inside a hot station house, it was time to go.

"We'll be in touch," Super Mario sneered, fumbling through a stack of paperwork.

We'll be in touch? Why would there be a need for him to be in touch? I told this asshole everything I knew about this case and never wanted to deal with him again.

After weighing the evidence, the duty captain placed the off-duty cop on modified assignment. Relieved of his gun and shield, the young cop was reassigned to the court system until the NYPD decided what to do with him.

I felt terrible starting an advance on the young patrolman. But he didn't help himself with that ridiculous story. Back at my office, everyone knew what had transpired and tried to cheer me up.

"Vic, your hands were tied. What were you supposed to do?" or, "Do you have a desk at IAB now?" were tossed at me by my sarcastic coworkers.

A few weeks later, my lieutenant called me into his office. "This afternoon, a lieutenant from IAB is stopping by to talk to you about that off-duty cop with the stolen SUV," he said.

"Lieutenant, I provided him with everything he needs to investigate the case," I said.

"It's probably a formality or something he doesn't understand," my lieutenant explained.

"Lou, I have a history with this guy, and it isn't good. I'd appreciate it if you were here when he stops by," I replied.

In my book *Grand Theft Auto, The NYPD's Auto Crime Division,* I discuss my lieutenant, nicknamed Chumley, for his resemblance to Tennessee Tuxedo's sidekick. Chumley thrived on conflict and relished in battling with the dark side.

"Yeah, maybe I'll hang around," Chumley chuckled, twirling his thick, dyed mustache.

If Chumley played poker, I would have owned him. Whenever he found something amusing, he'd start pulling on that ridiculous mustache.

Super Mario arrived for the sit-down dressed for a Jimmy Buffett concert. I could tell by the look on Chumley's face he didn't hold the IAB lieutenant in high regard based on his age and preppy attire.

We stepped into Chumley's office, where he shut the door for a little privacy. After the two lieutenants made small talk, Super Mario turned to me and said: "How is your investigation going?"

"Excuse me?" I asked.

"What have you uncovered in your investigation?" Super Mario asked.

I turned to Chumley, who had a shit-eating grin. Chumley knew how the game was played because he had spent a few years in IAB as a supervisor before coming to the Auto Crime Division. He wanted to sit back and watch me go back and forth with the young lieutenant before he stepped into the ring.

"Lieutenant, I gave you everything you needed to investigate this case," I explained.

"There's a lot more work to be done with this investigation," Super Mario replied, digging through a thick accordion folder.

"Good luck with that," I replied.

Super Mario lifted his head and scowled. If looks could kill, I'd be in the cemetery as he turned to Chumley for help with his mouthy detective. Amused, Chumley smiled and started twirling his walrus mustache between his fingers as Super Mario came unglued.

"You're an expert in auto crime. It's your job to determine if this MOS is guilty of possessing a stolen vehicle," Super Mario said.

"Lieutenant, every NYPD facility has a sign that reads 'Police corruption can be reported to the Internal Affairs Bureau.' It doesn't say anywhere on that sign that I'm supposed to conduct the investigation," I replied.

Before Super Mario could answer, Chumley chuckled, "He's right."

Super Mario looked like he wanted to cry. It was obvious after several weeks, he didn't know what to do with this case. I'm guessing wherever he was hiding all those years studying for civil service exams, he never learned how to do his job. That was his problem, not mine. I was under no obligation to investigate this case for him.

"Mario, if you have a question about this case or don't understand something, ask. But Detective Ferrari will not investigate this case for you," Chumley added.

"Next week, I'm interviewing this cop under oath, and I want Detective Ferrari there to ask a few questions," Super Mario replied.

"I'm not doing that," I shouted.

Super Mario was out of control. Wanting me to investigate this case for him was bad enough. Expecting me to sit in on a formal interview and question a cop facing departmental charges was above my pay grade. It was a ridiculous request that crossed many boundaries. My union would never allow it. They would fight that request tooth and nail, further stymieing the investigation.

"Mario, Mario, Mario, Detective Ferrari can't do that," Chumley laughed.

After a few tense moments, Chumley asked me to leave the room. The two lieutenants continued talking through the closed door as I returned to my desk. A few minutes later, Super Mario emerged from Chumley's office with a look of disappointment on his face.

"Good luck, Mario," Chumley said as the young lieutenant left our office with his tail between his legs.

"Well, you made another friend, Vic," Chumley snickered on his way to my desk.

"Lou, I'm under no obligation to help that jerk-off any more than I already have."

"Relax, Vic. I set him straight. But remember, you have another enemy," Chumley cautioned.

"Oh well," I replied.

"How many does that make now?" Chumley asked.

"I don't know. Too many to count," I replied.

Super Mario despised me from the courthouse incident. I might have been more forthcoming had he put his pride aside and asked for help instead of ordering me to do his bidding. The lightweight lieutenant thought he could walk into our office and order me to investigate his case. Those who work for the dark side are under the impression everyone will bow down to them. I was on solid legal ground and told him to piss off.

That was the last time I heard from Super Mario or the cop with the stolen Toyota Highlander. From my experience, it didn't look like the young cop had a leg to stand on. He'd have to explain why he purchased a new vehicle for thirty-five thousand dollars from a mechanic on Jerome Avenue instead of going to a Toyota dealership. That was going to be an uphill battle. He probably purchased the stolen SUV from a shady friend for ten thousand dollars cash with the promise he would keep his mouth shut if he got caught.

Whatever happened to the case is anyone's guess. The funny thing is all these years later, Super Mario turned up again. Now retired, he posts sophomoric comments on a NYPD Facebook group. My first reaction was to out him as the feckless supervisor he is. Then I thought, why should I get into an online pissing match with this jerkoff when I can write an entire story about him? Sometimes it's good to be a writer.

YO, FERRARI

In the twilight of my career, I was often tasked with teaching the new guys the ropes. I never enjoyed the assignment because I always had enough on my plate. I didn't have time to hold anyone's hand, but that's what Chumley wanted, so I obliged.

One winter evening, I was finishing an arrest with a newly assigned detective at the Bronx office.

After finishing our tour, we had to fill out a sign-out sheet and notify the main office in Queens that we were done for the day. After working several hours of overtime, I was exhausted and wanted to go home. I scribbled my name across the sign-out sheet before locking the office for the night.

Two hours later, I was lying in bed watching *Monday Night Football* when my phone rang.

Who the hell was calling me at eleven o'clock at night?

I snatched the cordless phone from its cradle and placed it beside my ear.

"Yo, Ferrari, where you at?" the voice said.

I knew the reason for the late-night call. I had forgotten to call the Queens office to sign out. The man on the phone was Lieutenant McKissick, the Auto Crime Division's integrity control officer or ICO. McKissick was a social climbing brown noser who belonged to every gladhanding organization in the department. Shriners, Freemasons, the Salvation Army. If there was a secret knock or handshake to get through the door, Lieutenant Illuminati knew about it.

The Illuminati's job was to ensure that everyone in the unit followed the rules. He kept watch on court appearances, overtime, and the sign-out sheet.

The Illuminati had lived a charmed life. He began his career in the comfy confines of Staten Island before networking himself into some of the NYPD's most coveted units. He never met an ass he didn't kiss while moving up the civil service ladder.

I didn't like the guy and did my best to stay out of his way.

"Hi, Lieutenant. How are you?" I asked.

"Ferrari, you and Detective Jenkins didn't sign out tonight."

"You're right, Lieutenant. We didn't. I'm sorry about that."

"That sign out sheet in the Bronx is just a formality. You're supposed to call the Queens base at the end of your tour," the Illuminati lectured.

I had worked in the unit longer than him and knew the procedure. He was right. I should have called the Queens office to sign out. But that didn't stop him from breaking my balls.

"Ferrari, I'm going to have to give you a command discipline (CD) for this," he added.

"Okay, Lieutenant," I replied, trying to concentrate on the football game.

"You guys in the Bronx can't come and go as you please," the Illuminati taunted.

It was bad enough calling me at eleven o'clock at night over a minor infraction, but now he's rubbing it in my face. After several minutes of listening to this nonsense, I cut him off.

"Excuse me, Lieutenant, but is there anything else?"

There was a moment of silence, followed by a heavy exhale. I had interrupted the Illuminati's sermon, and he wasn't happy about it.

"As I was saying, I'm going to write you up over this."

"I understand, Lieutenant. But it's past eleven o'clock, and I have to get up for work tomorrow," I replied before hanging up on him.

I sat in my bed, staring at the phone in my hand. I was pissed. Giving me a command discipline for not signing out was stretching it. But to call me at home to give me a lecture was sticking in the knife and twisting it. This could have waited till morning, but he wanted me to know he was in charge. Lieutenant Illuminati loved to tease and embarrass underlings until they pushed back. Then, he'd pull rank. Respecting someone who smacks you in the face from the other side of the fence is a tough pill to swallow.

The following morning, I marched into Chumley's office. "Lieutenant, you have a minute?" I asked.

"What's up, Vic?" he asked, leaning back in his chair.

"I wanted to give you the head's up that you'll be hearing from Lieutenant Mckissik today."

"Oh, and why is that?" Chumley asked with a curious look.

"Last night, after finishing up with a collar, I forgot to call the Queens base to sign out."

"So?" Chumley asked.

"Well, Lieutenant Mckissik called my house at eleven o'clock last night to inform me that he's giving me and Jenkins command disciplines for not signing out," I explained.

"He called you at eleven o'clock to tell you that?" Chumley asked.

"Yup," I replied.

"Some people have to justify their existence," Chumley grumbled, reaching for the phone.

"Lou, Jenkins is new here and doesn't know the procedure. It's my fault. I'll take the CD," I said.

"Doesn't this fucking guy have enough to do in Queens without bothering my detectives?" Chumley grumbled.

Chumley gritted his teeth while pushing buttons on his desktop phone. I knew he wasn't a fan of the Illuminati, so he might intervene on my behalf.

"Vic, close the door and keep quiet," Chumley said as the phone rang.

"Hey Mike. It's Kevin."

After exchanging pleasantries, Lieutenant Illuminati told Chumley about my misgivings the night before.

"Well, that's why I'm calling. Ferrari told me all about it," Chumley explained.

They went back and forth with Chumley laughing a few times before taking control of the conversation.

"Mike, Mike, listen to me. You remind me of a highway cop with a one-track mind."

I could only hear one end of the conversation, but that wasn't a compliment. Highway cops are not known for their discretion, issuing moving violations to the majority of motorists they stop.

"Mike, let me give you an analogy you might understand. You got my guy pulled over to the side of the road at eleven o'clock at night for a broken taillight while you have over a hundred detectives in that Queens office robbing you blind," Chumley explained.

I almost laughed when Chumley chided the Illuminati.

"Listen, Mike, I'm not asking. I'm telling you to leave Ferrari alone," Chumley said before hanging up the phone.

"I guess I have another enemy?" I asked.

"You sure do. I suggest staying out of Lieutenant McKissick's way for a while," Chumley cautioned.

"Lou, every time I come to you with a problem with a supervisor, it seems to get worse," I kidded.

"Vic, either work on your people skills or study for the sergeant's exam," Chumley replied.

"Are you speaking from experience?" I asked.

"Vic, don't let the door hit you in the ass," Chumley replied.

I had my difficulties with Chumley, but I'll say this about the man: he always backed his detectives and never took shit from anybody. Chumley was a throwback to the golden years of the NYPD. He spent twenty years working in busy precincts before taking the sergeant's exam. Chumley saw Lieutenant Illuminati as someone who hadn't earned his stripes.

Supervisors like Lieutenant Illuminati are a product of a flawed civil service system. No matter how many times they screw up, all is forgiven once promoted up the civil service ladder. Every rung you climb is a baptism that washes away your sins.

After retiring from the NYPD, I worked for a small police department in Florida. To become a supervisor, you had to work the street for several years before taking the sergeant's exam. A review board also put your career under a microscope to determine if you possessed the qualities to be a supervisor.

I realize that kind of scrutiny is not practical for the New York City Police Department, where sometimes dozens of supervisors are promoted at a time.

While some NYPD members are up to the task, others have no business supervising men and women making life-and-death decisions. Ultimately, it is the hardworking cops and detectives who pay the price for these clueless sycophants' quest for power.

CHAPTER 2

THEY DON'T MAKE IT EASY FOR YOU

The day I got hired by the New York City Police Department, I was told not to speak to the news media. "If a reporter asks for a comment, politely refer them to the Deputy Commissioner of Public Information" was the standard line.

Long before cops began seeking publicity dancing around like jackasses on TikTok, mum was the word. NYPD members were instructed to keep their mouths shut for fear of embarrassing the department. It was understood that nothing good could come from speaking to the press. The NYPD does not trust reporters. And for a good reason. In today's climate, the news media rarely publishes a favorable story about law enforcement.

The New York City Police Department and the press have always had a cantankerous relationship. It starts at three a.m. when news trucks start to rumble through New York City's five boroughs. Delivery drivers, like reporters, have deadlines. Before the morning commute, they drop thick bundles of ink-stained paper at newsstands. Most midnight cops look the other way when a newspaper truck rolls through a red light to keep on schedule. When spotted, the delivery truck slows to a crawl long enough to lower a few warm newspapers to the pursuing patrol car. Nothing is said during the five-mile-per-hour transaction before each party goes its separate way. As a rookie, I learned the hard way what happens when you write a news truck a red light summons.

"Hey, kid, why did you bang the news truck?" the old-timer shouted across the precinct locker room.

"He blew a red light," I replied.

I was in the precinct less than a week before I got my first scolding at the hands of a salty hair bag who didn't want to pay for his newspaper.

"We don't write newspaper trucks," he said.

"Why not?" I asked.

"You like paying for the newspaper?" the middle-aged cop asked.

"It's a quarter," I replied.

"Listen, smartass, leave the newspaper trucks alone," he instructed.

I was confused. All I heard from day one was the press wasn't a friend of law enforcement. Now this cheap bastard was giving me shit for writing up a delivery driver. The New York City media relishes the opportunity to bash the NYPD. Silly me, I thought I had scored one for our side, and this schmuck tells me to back off.

It was then I realized the New York City Police Department and the media depend on and despise each other.

When detectives hit a dead end, they'll turn to the press in hopes of stirring up leads. Reporters on a deadline will call their police contacts for comment. Despite the working arrangement, they don't trust each other. A slip of the tongue from a rookie cop guarding a crime scene can provide explosive content that runs for days. Most NYPD members want nothing to do with the press. However, a small percentage will provide these unscrupulous provocateurs with confidential information. Some are paid moles hiding in the bowels of One Police Plaza.

These Judases know the department's temperature because they've buried their nose in the ass of everyone above the rank of captain. Others have an ax to grind. They don't like their boss or feel they got passed over for a cushy assignment. Every NYPD command has a couple of malcontents looking to even the score. Hell has no fury like an empty suit that thinks they've been slighted. Unfortunately, those who do the least complain the most when things don't go their way.

Early in my NYPD career, I saw what happens when cops run their mouths to the news media. The first specialized unit I worked in had just gone through a massive personnel purge. Veteran cops padding their pensions had racked up massive amounts of arrest overtime that caught the attention of the Bronx borough. To combat the collars for dollars phenomena, the bean counters at the borough sent a hatchet man to clean house. The new commanding officer followed his orders to the letter. He changed tours, split up partners, and dumped cops from specialized units.

As the veteran cops retired or transferred out of the once proud unit, it got restocked with rookie cops. The few old-timers who survived the bloodbath were bitter and vindictive. With morale at an all-time low, the old-timers started a work action to push back against the borough's heavy-handed treatment.

NYPD members are forbidden to organize or take part in a strike. A summons slowdown is a different matter. Although legal, organizing a summons slowdown is a surefire way to end your NYPD career. New York City takes the millions of dollars generated from parking and moving violations seriously.

When summons numbers are down, One Police Plaza goes into panic mode. Shit runs downhill at the New York City Police Department when the police commissioner takes a dump on his borough commander. Now sporting a brown hat, the borough commander invites the precinct's commanding officer over for a friendly chat. After leaving the meeting covered in feces, the precinct commander threatens everyone in his command that heads will roll for participating in a summons slowdown.

You shouldn't take it personally when your squad sergeant informs you your summons activity is not up to par. He isn't receiving a commission for the parking tickets you write. He's only the messenger. The man chosen to deliver the message was a well-respected twenty-five-year member of the department.

I always found the senior sergeant to be a fair man. A veteran of the 1970s riots, the grizzled supervisor carried an ax handle instead of a nightstick and never wore his bulletproof vest. Long before passing the sergeant's exam, the former Harlem cop had survived a gun battle, earning him the prestigious Combat Cross Medal. He never spoke of the incident that left his adversary dead. "He's gone, and I'm still here," was his response when someone asked.

Two weeks into the summons slowdown, the battle-hardened supervisor walked to the podium to address the troops for roll call. "Everyone, please take a seat," he asked, skipping uniform inspection. The stoic sergeant rarely said much, but when he spoke, everyone listened. "Listen, I'm not going to play games with you guys," E.F. Hutton said, looking around the crowded room. The contrite sergeant gripped both sides of the podium and stared at the ceiling for guidance before proceeding with the intervention.

"There was a summons quota when I came on this job twenty-five years ago. There's a summons quota today, and they'll be one long after I'm gone," the sergeant said.

There was no acknowledgment or denial from the cops in the room waiting for the other shoe to drop. "This guy isn't playing around," the sergeant warned, pointing to the ceiling at the commanding officer's second-floor office.

That was obvious by the endless nitpicking at the hands of borough stooges brought in to ensure punishment was doled out daily.

"If you guys don't want to write summons, don't write them. I'm not the guy looking to hurt anyone. But plenty of supervisors here will," the sergeant said.

The warning was delivered. Get back to writing tickets, or there'll be another round of misery. On the surface, nobody took the sergeant's warning personally. He didn't want to see anyone get hurt.

Luckily for me, probationary cops were exempt from the slowdown.

After roll call, I sat back and watched the veteran cops debate the pros and cons of the unsanctioned work action in the precinct parking lot.

"Whoever goes back to writing summonses is a pussy," shouted our loudmouth union delegate.

"Fuck you. If I lose my steady days off, I don't have anyone to watch my kids after school," another cop snapped.

"We all have to make sacrifices," the delegate snapped back.

"Are you kidding me? You get paid to represent us and enjoy the protection of the PBA (Patrolmen's Benevolent Association). What sacrifices are you making?" the irate cop shouted back.

The arguing went back and forth before punches were thrown. Like a pimple ready to pop, it was only a matter of time before someone got marked with an unsightly blemish.

A few days later, the local newspaper published an article about our summons slowdown. It stated that cops in a Bronx command were unhappy with their commanding officer and refused to write summonses. The story also stated that despite its denials, the New York City Police Department had a summons quota for its uniformed members.

What the article got wrong was what the sergeant said to the outgoing platoon. Someone lied or took the warning out of context before passing it along to a columnist who did a hit piece on the sergeant. The article implied that the well-respected supervisor had ordered his cops to paper the streets with tickets or face serious consequences. The story failed to mention that the warning came from One Police Plaza.

A week later, I was tasked with driving the besmirched sergeant. He sat silent for the first few hours, gazing out the window in a perpetual fog. About halfway through our shift, he uttered, "Whoever called that reporter has ruined my career."

I was a rookie cop and didn't know what to say to the decorated sergeant who shared with me what it was like to get raked over the coals by the New York City media.

"My son's teacher asked him why his father is ordering cops to write tickets," he fumed.

Before I could think of a sympathetic reply, the sergeant continued to vent.

"My neighbors read the paper. They must think I'm the biggest scumbag in the world," he complained.

"Do you know who did it?" I asked.

"I have a pretty good idea," the sergeant replied, sipping his coffee.

A few weeks after the article hit the newsstands, the sergeant quietly filed for retirement. Those who knew him said he would have hung around for a while had his good name not been ruined. There wasn't a gold watch or retirement party commemorating a quarter-century of service.

He left and never said goodbye. Six months after his self-imposed exile, the precinct club tried to reward the vilified sergeant with a retirement plaque. Repeated calls to his house went unanswered while the plaque gathered dust on a shelf. The message was clear. After a twenty-five-year career in law enforcement, the respected sergeant was done with the New York City Police Department.

Most NYPD members want nothing to do with the news media. Whether it's a cold shoulder at a crime scene or the occasional parking ticket slapped over a press parking permit, there's no love lost between these two entities.

When reporters want to break a story, they don't care how many lives they have to ruin to get it. Love him or hate him, Rush Limbaugh coined the phrase "drive-by media" to describe a reckless press core that riddles its target with a myriad of accusations before moving on to the next victim. I understand it's a reporter's job to cover a newsworthy story. But most columnists are on a search and destroy mission when covering law enforcement.

During my tenure with the NYPD, the crime reporters were the most egregious storytellers.

Police work is a dangerous game. Unfortunately, cops and robbers sometimes exchange gunfire. After a police shooting, a pack of rabid hyenas descends into the neighborhood looking for a story. Instead of getting to the bottom of what happened, reporters dig for the deceased's middle school graduation photo to show that it's open season on altar boys. Fair and impartial goes out the window when the news media wants its pound of flesh.

Rarely do these so-called journalists have a kind word for the brave men and women of the NYPD who risk their lives daily. Instead, they trawl the gutters, searching for street hustlers with a story to sell. Most of their stories focus on race and exaggerated tales of police brutality.

Even on the rare occasion when they get a story right, they run it for days, fanning the flames of a smoldering city, hoping to win a Pulitzer Prize. These storytellers believe themselves to be the moral arbiters of society despite their political bias. A few lines into their columns, you are knee-deep in shit, wading through a dark alley in search of that reluctant source.

They'd like you to believe they write their columns between sips of whisky in a rough part of town. In reality, they are tucked away in a Starbucks in Red Hook, tapping away on their Macs, lecturing the working class about social responsibility. Repent and recycle, Ivy League brats warn, before the world comes to an end.

Before cell phones and laptops, newspapers littered NYPD precincts. Every morning before roll call, the outgoing platoon sat around the muster room, thumbing through a copy of one of New York City's periodicals. Unfortunately, those days are long gone. Print cannot compete with digital technology. Today, stories are churned out in real time and revised before our eyes. The old-school reporter who hung around the courthouse waiting for the perp walk was replaced by a Twitter-addicted snowflake. The more things change, the more they remain the same. The news media was just as full of shit then as it is now.

THE COST OF DOING BUSINESS

The 4x12 shift is fast-paced with lots of action. Between the bar fights and domestic violence calls, criminals are jumping into the back seats of patrol cars. Unfortunately, the NYPD and the powers that be running the criminal justice system do everything they can to make life difficult for street cops. The department treats arrests as a burden or inconvenience because the moment a cop puts handcuffs on someone, one fewer patrol car is available to answer radio runs.

Unfortunately, some supervisors discourage cops from making quality of life arrests.

"Jesus Christ, Ferrari, you think this bullshit drug arrest is going to make a difference?" one sergeant asked after I brought in a drug dealer with a bag filled with crack cocaine.

When I tried to explain that there was a line of crackheads leading up to the dealer, the sergeant shouted, "Great, now I have to pick up jobs tonight!"

I never thought I was saving the city. I just wanted to do my job. Redundant paperwork, restrictions on overtime, and the lack of transportation to and from the courthouse are designed to make you think twice about making an arrest. At the time, I was young and idealistic. I wasn't deterred by petty obstacles while leading my precinct in arrests.

I knew they wouldn't make it easy, but I didn't care. What's the point of being a cop if you don't arrest the bad guys? During my NYPD career, I made over six hundred arrests and was involved in thousands of others. I didn't mind the sleepless nights, tour changes, or the army of ball-busting paper-pushers whose job was to slow me down. After a while, I learned the tricks of the trade and navigated my way through the criminal justice system, despite its many roadblocks.

If you walk into an NYPD precinct during the afternoon, you'll notice a bunch of smiling baby-faced twenty-olds standing around in police uniforms.

As a young cop, I was no different, racing around the precinct chasing the radio. I loved the job, especially making arrests. One spring evening, my partner and I were on patrol near Van Cortlandt Park when the radio came to life. A robbery five minutes ago on Broadway. The perp had forced his way into an elderly woman's apartment before fleeing with her jewelry.

"Central, do you have a description of the perp?" my partner asked over his portable radio.

"The perp is a white male, early twenties, with shoulder-length blond hair, blue eyes, and an overbite," the dispatcher replied.

"He sounds like Tom Petty," my partner mocked.

I drove up and down Broadway, crisscrossing through side streets, searching for the elusive rockstar robber.

"We were around the corner when the job came over. Where the fuck did he go?" my partner asked.

"You know where we haven't looked?" I replied, pointing to the entrance ramp of the Henry Hudson Parkway.

"It's worth a try," my partner said as I merged onto the narrow two-lane parkway.

We hadn't traveled a hundred yards when I saw a skinny white guy with long blond hair hitchhiking on the side of the road.

"Tom Petty," I shouted.

"Where?" my partner asked.

"Look at the guy hitchhiking," I said, turning on the vehicle's emergency lights.

When the lights came on, Tom Petty looked like he wanted to run offstage and into the woods of the Henry Hudson Parkway.

"Eric, do not get out of the car when I pull up to him," I said.

"Why not?" my partner asked.

"I don't want him running into the woods. I'm going to give him a bullshit story about a lost child. When he leans into the car, grab his arm, and I'll jump out and cuff him," I explained.

As I pulled onto the shoulder of the roadway, Tom Petty lit a cigarette. This was a good sign. The Heartbreaker frontman was hoping to talk his way out of this.

"Hey, buddy, we're looking for a lost child," I shouted out the passenger window."

"I haven't seen a kid out here," he replied, puffing on his cigarette.

Tom Petty was a nervous wreck, wiping beads of sweat from his grimy face. I had to play this right, or it was off to the races.

"Let me show you a photo," I said, combing through a pile of paperwork on the front seat.

The Traveling Wilbury relaxed, stepping towards the radio car. "Get ready, Eric," I whispered to my partner.

Lowering his head, the disheveled hitchhiker leaned into the car as I handed him a piece of paper. He let his guard down long enough for my partner to clamp down on his arm when I jumped out of the driver's seat and raced around the radio car.

"Vic, hurry. I can't hold him much longer," my partner shouted, grappling with the suspect.

I grabbed the sweaty perp around the shoulder before spreading him across the hood of our radio car.

"It's over," I shouted, placing him in handcuffs.

A few minutes later, a police car arrived with an elderly woman seated in the back.

"That's the son of a bitch!" she shouted, climbing out of the police car.

I dug through the rock star's pockets and pulled out a large diamond engagement ring.

"Is this your ring?" I asked the elderly victim.

"My late husband, Norman, gave that to me in 1942," she said.

"I'm guessing you'd like to press charges?"

"Are you shitting me?" the elderly woman barked.

At the station house, I learned the young punk had quite the criminal resume. Tom Petty had a rap sheet several pages long filled with arrests. No one is lower on the criminal totem pole than those who prey on the elderly. Senior citizens are excellent victims because of their inability to identify their assailants. Fortunately for me, the eighty-something-year-old woman had twenty-twenty vision.

"How bad does it look for me?" Tom Petty asked while I was driving him to Central Booking.

"Bad," I replied.

"How bad?" he said.

"You robbed an eighty-year-old woman. You're going upstate this time," I explained.

After lodging the scumbag at Bronx Central Booking, I ran home for a few hours of sleep. There was no benefit in making a late arrest on the 4x12 shift. If you don't submit your paperwork to pre-arraignment before they close, you must return at seven a.m. the following morning. It's a hard kick in the ass for a job well done. I never saw the point of letting a bad guy go because of a few hours of lost sleep. The following morning, I met with a district attorney to file charges against Tom Petty.

"I need you to testify before the grand jury on Friday," the young prosecutor said, digging through a drawer for a subpoena.

"If you want me here Friday, send that to my precinct," I instructed.

"I'm giving you the subpoena now," the naïve district attorney said, handing me a slip of paper.

"Listen, you can hand me the Ten Commandments on a stone tablet. I'm still not going to be here Friday. Send that subpoena to my precinct," I replied.

As a precinct cop, I couldn't attend court without my administrative lieutenant's approval. The district attorney had to send the subpoena to the precinct, where it would sit on some flunky's desk for days, waiting to be reviewed. It's a poorly managed game of telephone that leaves everyone pointing fingers at each other when no one shows up to court.

"Send a subpoena to my command, and I'll be here," I said before heading home to catch some sleep.

The following afternoon, I walked into the roll call office and asked a burned-out police administrative aide, or PAA, about the subpoena. I had just started my 4x12 shift and wanted to know what tour I'd be working on the following day. If the subpoena were there, I'd sign out at the end of my shit and return in the morning for court. No subpoena meant I'd come to work on Friday afternoon.

"Nope, no subpoena," she said, sifting through a thick stack of notifications.

"Are you sure? I should have grand jury tomorrow," I replied.

"Yes, Ferrari, I'm sure," the salty PAA shot back, banging the keys of her IBM typewriter.

I figured Tom Petty took a plea bargain. I wish the district attorney had given me the heads-up instead of ghosting me. That happens all the time. Unless you track down the prosecutor for the disposition, you will never know what happened to your case.

Later that evening, a Nissan 280Z blew through a stop sign and almost T-boned our radio car before racing off on Broadway. My partner gave chase while I ran the vehicle's license plate number.

"Eric, it's stolen," I said, as we pursued the Japanese import over the West 225 Street Bridge into Manhattan.

The driver lost control of his vehicle before crashing into an el pillar. The collision disabled the stolen car, enabling my partner and me to apprehend the driver. I returned the arrest to the Fiftieth Precinct in the Bronx, charging the perp with grand larceny auto.

On the surface, it was a simple stolen vehicle arrest. That was what I thought until the intake supervisor at Bronx Central Booking began breaking my balls over logistics.

"This is a Manhattan arrest," the sergeant said.

"No, Sarge, it originated in the Bronx," I replied.

"The arrest location is West 218th Street and Broadway," he said, pointing to the address on the online booking worksheet with his bony finger.

I was aware of what I wrote on the arrest report. The miserable midnight sergeant was splitting hairs because his jail cells were full. Rerouting my perp to Manhattan Central Booking would be one less thing he had to worry about. I had to convince this schmuck not to send me to Lower Manhattan to process the arrest. We debated geography for several minutes before I was overruled.

"Where are we going?" the confused prisoner asked when I pulled him from the crowded bullpen.

"The sergeant wants me to process your arrest in Manhattan," I replied.

"Oh good."

"Why is that good?"

"I live in Manhattan," the prisoner explained.

"I'm glad we could accommodate you," I mocked.

Like the Bronx, it was a busy night at Manhattan Central Booking. Outside was a line of cops and prisoners waiting to enter the building. It took almost three hours to lodge my car thief and file the paperwork for tomorrow's consultation with a Manhattan district attorney. After a long evening, I signed out and headed home for a few hours of sleep. When I returned to the precinct the following morning, I got blindsided by my administrative lieutenant.

"Hey, Ferrari, you have grand jury today," he said, handing me a court notification.

The lanky lackey was the consummate company man, following the patrol guide to the letter. He spent his days creeping around the station house, trafficking in precinct gossip. I never made his Christmas card list because I refused to kiss his ass.

"Lieutenant, I asked about this subpoena yesterday and was told it hadn't arrived," I said.

"Ferrari, what do you want me to tell you? It's here now," he replied, handing me the slip of paper.

"Lieutenant, I made an arrest in Manhattan last night," I explained.

"So?"

"So? I can't be in two places at the same time," I replied.

"Well, when you're done with the Manhattan arrest, head up to the Bronx courthouse and take care of the other case."

"Can I take a radio car?" I asked.

"Sorry, Ferrari, we're short on cars. Take the iron horse (subway)," the administrative lieutenant explained.

Every NYPD precinct has assholes like this guy. There were plenty of radio cars in the precinct parking lot. The sniveling worm didn't want to make an entry in the command log. It was easier for him to send me across the city on a crowded subway train in my uniform. After processing my arrest in Manhattan, he expected me to race uptown to the Bronx courthouse to testify.

"Lieutenant, can I change into my civilian clothes?" I asked.

"Absolutely not," he replied.

It was obvious my administrative lieutenant wasn't sympathetic to my plight. The lazy son of a bitch never got involved with anything that cost him a good night's sleep.

I didn't want to give him the satisfaction of seeing that I was upset, so I nodded and walked away.

"Hey, Ferrari, I'm not paying you overtime. Be back by three o'clock," he instructed.

It was impossible for me to travel the city by subway, testify in two boroughs, and be back at the precinct by three o'clock. I would need a cape to pull that off. My administrative lieutenant knew this wasn't humanly possible. He was making sure I wouldn't submit an overtime slip.

"Sure, Lou," I replied, heading to the precinct parking lot.

Fuck him. I'll take my car to court, I thought, digging into my pocket for the keys to my Nissan Sentra.

The NYPD forbids its members from using their private vehicles on duty. You can lose up to five vacation days for violating the ridiculous rule. I'd also have to be careful parking around the Manhattan courthouse. A mistake could lead to an expensive parking ticket, not to mention the possibility of getting towed.

After three hours of sleep, the last thing I wanted was a subway ride into Lower Manhattan. Taking my car was worth the risk. Just as I was about to put the key in the door lock, something told me to turn around. Standing behind me with his arms folded was my creepy administrative lieutenant. The rat bastard had followed me into the precinct parking lot and was looking to stick one in my ass for taking my car to court. Undeterred, I opened the door, pretending to be looking for something inside my vehicle, when he approached.

"Hey, Ferrari, I hope you don't think you're taking your car to court," he said.

"No, boss, I'm looking for a pen," I replied, digging through my glove compartment.

He watched my every move until I left the parking lot and headed up Broadway toward the train station. Riding the subway is a pain in the ass. Riding the subway in a police uniform is full-blown hemorrhoids.

You can't sit because you're expected to stand, and everyone wants to talk to you. Half asleep, I grabbed a handrail while chatty straphangers peppered me with questions during the hour-long ride into Lower Manhattan.

Once downtown, I clocked into Manhattan pre-arraignment before taking a seat in the crowded complaint room.

NYPD members can spend days in the complaint room before speaking to a district attorney. The volume of arrests that come through the Manhattan court system is staggering. Defendants sometimes have to wait several days before they see a judge. After several hours of waiting, I became worried. I couldn't afford to sit around killing time while last week's robbery arrest hung in the balance. If I didn't make it uptown to testify, the robbery suspect would walk. I made my way to the basket containing last night's arrest folders and sweet-talked a secretary into moving my folder to the top of the file. A few minutes later, an assistant district attorney called me to her cubicle to discuss last night's stolen car arrest.

"This arrest should be prosecuted in the Bronx," the young assistant district attorney said, reviewing the folder.

"I agree with you. But they ordered me to take it to Manhattan," I replied.

I knew this was going to happen. The idiot sergeant from Bronx Central Booking had passed the buck, and I was getting the antlers.

If the Manhattan district attorney's office refused to prosecute the case, I'd have to pull the prisoner out of the cells again and take him back to the Bronx, hoping they'd deal with it there.

"Let me speak to my supervisor," she said, excusing herself from the cubicle.

For several nerve-wracking minutes, I waited for the other shoe to drop. Most likely, they would send the case back to the Bronx.

"Officer Ferrari, today is your lucky day," the young DA said, returning to her desk. I didn't feel lucky with little sleep and an empty stomach. But I'd take what I could get.

An hour later, I was on an uptown 4 train headed back to the Bronx.

One down, one to go, I thought, grabbing a hot dog in front of the Bronx courthouse. Inside, I waded through a sea of cops and criminals before taking the elevator up to the grand jury bureau.

"We have a problem," the nervous district attorney said as I entered his office.

The prosecutor explained my victim needed transportation to the courthouse. If she didn't testify, the case would get dismissed. Tom Petty would walk, undeterred by a turnstile criminal justice system.

"What do you want to do?" I asked.

"Would you mind driving up to Riverdale and bringing her here?" the district attorney asked.

"I don't have a vehicle."

"Oh, that's okay. You can take a pool car," the district attorney replied.

Pool car? Is he kidding me?

My precinct parking lot was filled with police cars I couldn't use. This guy knows me for five minutes and trusts me with a "pool car."

He didn't have to ask twice before I jumped into a late model gray Ford Taurus and headed to West 263rd Street and Broadway to pick up my elderly complainant.

When I arrived, I had to coax the reluctant victim from her apartment. Unbeknownst to me, she was terrified of Tom Petty, who roughed her up while forcing his way into her apartment.

I assured the eighty-something-year-old woman Tom Petty was cooling his heels in jail, provided she told her story to a Bronx grand jury. After convincing her everything would be all right, she agreed to accompany me to the courthouse.

"How do I look?" she asked, waiting outside the grand jury room.

"Like Geraldine Page," I replied, causing her to blush.

"They're ready," the district attorney said, poking his head out of the grand jury room.

Bronx grand juries are famous for dismissing cases. In boroughs like Queens, Manhattan, and Staten Island, the grand jury panels are more cop-friendly, where indictments are handed out like lollipops at the pediatrician's office.

In the Bronx and Brooklyn, you'll often see half the grand jury panel dozing off or rolling their eyes during witness testimony.

I felt good about our chances of getting an indictment because it was a solid case.

A few minutes later, the elderly victim stepped from the grand jury room. "That was fun," she said.

"Fun?" I laughed.

"It was just like *Law & Order*. I placed my hand on the Bible and swore to tell the truth, the whole truth, and nothing but the truth," she giggled.

I was glad Granny was having a good time, but my day was far from over. I still had to drive her back to Riverdale before returning the pool car to the district attorney's office. Then, I had to figure out how to get back to the precinct before three p.m. The NYPD is quite frugal with court overtime.

I could hand in an overtime slip, but it wouldn't be worth my time. It would take weeks before it showed up in my check while my integrity control officer dragged his feet, asking for movement sheets and memo book entries.

Several seconds later, the district attorney came bouncing out of the grand jury room with a smile. "True bill," he said.

The grand jury voted to indict. Tom Petty wasn't going anywhere.

On the ride back to Riverdale, Grandma Moses held on for dear life as I sliced through traffic on the Major Deegan Expressway.

"Do you always drive like this?" she asked after I slammed the brakes in front of her building.

"I'm sorry if I scared you," I replied, helping the octogenarian out of the vehicle.

"Scared? I haven't had this much fun in decades," she laughed.

I thanked Granny for her cooperation before racing down Broadway en route to the Bronx Courthouse.

Broadway, from West 242nd Street to the Yonkers border, is a four-lane roadway tucked between rows of six-story red brick condominiums and Van Cortlandt Park. The sprawling park doubles as an after-school hangout for teenagers.

While waiting at a traffic light, I noticed a rust-colored Toyota Celica filled with teens pull up to the park.

The inexperienced driver had difficulty parallel parking the Japanese import, ramming two vehicles before winding up on the sidewalk. Watching the spectacle unfold, I decided to run the vehicle's license plate over my portable radio.

What am I doing?

If the car was stolen, I'd have four juvenile arrests and a lot of explaining to do. Four arrests meant at least six hours of overtime. My penny-pinching administrative lieutenant wouldn't like that. While I weighed my options, the dispatcher began raising me over the radio.

"Five-O portable. What's your location?" the dispatcher asked.

"West 252nd Street and Broadway," I replied.

"Five-O portable. That vehicle is stolen," the dispatcher said.

"Can you send another unit over here?" I asked.

I sat tight and waited for the cavalry to arrive. I didn't want to risk a car chase into neighboring Yonkers. A few minutes later, several radio cars surrounded the stolen Toyota.

My coworkers teased me while pulling the four stoned teens from the stolen vehicle.

"Ferrari, when Lieutenant Smithfield see's this, he's going to shit twice and bark at the moon," one cop laughed.

"Fuck him. He doesn't pay my bills," I replied.

I followed the caravan of police cars back to the precinct, where I found my administrative lieutenant waiting for me in the parking lot.

"Ferrari, what the fuck is this?" he shouted as I led two handcuffed teens out of the back of a radio car.

"Four juvenile arrests for GLA (grand larceny auto)," I replied.

"You're supposed to be at court. What were you doing at Van Cortlandt Park?"

"I had to drive a witness home, and on the way back, I ran into them," I explained, pointing to the teens.

"Wait a minute. I watched you get on the subway this morning. Whose fucking car is this?" he asked, prompting my two juvenile car thieves to laugh.

"I borrowed it from the DA's office," I replied, walking the teens into the station house.

Cops hate juvenile arrests. There's lots of paperwork, and the procedure changes every fifteen minutes. There are countless phone calls to different agencies to determine if your juvenile is spending the night at Bronx Central Booking, Spofford (kiddie jail), or can be released to their parents.

The first to arrive to pick up their child was a middle-aged couple from Yonkers. After introducing themselves, the husband asked to speak to me in the hallway.

"Listen, can you help me out?" he asked, reaching into his back pocket.

"Excuse me?" I asked.

"I'm on the job in Yonkers," he replied, handing me his police identification card.

I felt a knot in the pit of my stomach. Cops do favors for each other all the time. Parking tickets and moving violations are virtually nonexistent between law enforcement agencies. But I knew the next thing that would come out of his mouth was something I couldn't do.

"Can you do something about my son's arrest?"

"I'm sorry, but I can't."

"Look, my son is a good kid. He didn't know the car was stolen," the father explained.

"Did your son mention he had a screwdriver in his pocket to start the car?" I asked.

I felt bad for the father and didn't want to come off like an asshole. But I couldn't let him guilt me into voiding his son's arrest.

"I'm sorry, but I can't help you," I replied before returning to the juvenile room.

Inside the tiny room, the Yonkers cop's wife was screaming at her son.

"What do you have to say for yourself?" she shouted into the boy's face.

Humiliated, the juvenile car thief attempted to save face by letting out a snicker.

"You think this is funny?" his mother shouted.

The snarky teen rolled his eyes, prompting the statuesque woman to jump from her chair and lunge for a stapler on a desk. Before anyone could react, the enraged woman pried open the foot-long stapler and plunged it into the side of her son's arm.

"Mama, I'm sorry!" the boy screamed.

"Let me show you how funny it is," she shouted, driving staples into the boy's shoulder.

The hysterical woman had to be pulled off her son and dragged out of the room by her husband. After everything calmed down, I told the bleeding juvenile delinquent to consider spending the night at Spofford.

A few minutes later, my administrative lieutenant summoned me to his office.

"Ferrari, why is it that everything you touch turns into a three-ring circus?" he asked.

"Lieutenant?" I replied before he interrupted.

"You're not supposed to be riding around by yourself fighting crime!" he shouted.

He was pissed, and some form of punishment was coming. I'd probably wind up on the midnights with the old-timers and drunks staggering out of the bars on Broadway.

Midnights are fun every once in a while. But to work them steady sucks the life out of you. The graveyard shift has few advantages besides the free newspaper from a passing news truck. While my enraged administrative lieutenant read me the riot act, our commanding officer came barreling into the office. The burly Polish deputy inspector was an unpredictable character with the attention span of a toddler. We called him the Mad Hatter because you never knew what he would do next.

In my book *The NYPD's Flying Circus, Cops, Crime & Chaos*, I share how he once ordered me to transport a dead coyote to the Bronx Zoo in the trunk of a radio car. Another time, he had me searching for polka music and an accordion player for an upcoming barbecue.

"Smithfield, I need you to assign more cops on the day shift to combat this auto theft problem," the Mad Hatter shouted, waving a sheet of paper filled with statistics.

"Inspector, can you give me a couple of minutes?" the administrative lieutenant asked, pointing at me.

Ignoring his lackey, the Mad Hatter carried on. "I'm getting killed with stolen cars at the north end of the precinct," he shouted.

That was my cue. "Inspector, I just collared four teenagers in a stolen car by Van Cortlandt Park."

The raving lunatic lit up like a pinball machine and threw his beefy arm around my shoulder.

"You have to be kidding me? That's fucking great," the Mad Hatter shouted. I had my administrative lieutenant by the balls. How could he punish me while the commanding officer was singing my praises?

"I need more cops like you around here," the Mad Hatter proclaimed.

My administrative lieutenant looked like someone had taken a shit in his Easter basket while the Polish precinct commander rambled on: "Hey, Maserati, how about I give you a computer car and weekends off, and you hunt car thieves for me?" he asked.

"Thank you, Inspector. I won't let you down," I said, shaking his hand.

My administrative lieutenant stared at me in disbelief. In the blink of an eye, I went from the midnight shift to a tit detail. And there wasn't a thing he could do about it. I might have won the battle, but a long war was ahead. For the next few years, I played a dangerous game of cat and mouse with my administrative lieutenant. Whenever a parade, strike, or demonstration came up, I got pulled from my assignment and sent over for the day. It happened so often that my coworkers would tease that I had millions of frequent flyer miles traveling around New York City's five boroughs.

During my twenty-year NYPD career, I often had to improvise when obstacles got in my way. Countless court appearances, ridiculous rules, and a bureaucracy were designed to keep me from doing my job. Looking back, I didn't care. It was the cost of doing business.

CHAPTER 3

IS THIS LEGAL?

Is this legal? That's a question I got asked many times during my NYPD career. Everyone, including my family and friends, thought I possessed the legal mind of Alan Dershowitz. Six months of criminal law at the police academy isn't the same as passing the bar exam. If you wear a police uniform, get a retainer because of the countless legal questions.

Everyone expects the police to have all the answers to their legal issues. Criminal, civil, and bankruptcy, I wasn't qualified to weigh in on most of the ridiculous questions thrown my way. People love to solicit advice from a cop. It costs nothing to ask, and when something goes wrong, it's your fault. "Do you want to go to jail?" I'd ask after listening to some crackpot's half-baked scheme. NYPD members aren't exempt from making poor life decisions. You wouldn't believe the stupid ideas I'd hear getting tossed around the precinct locker room. Everything from shady tax preparers to multi-level marketing pyramid schemes would sweep through the station house like the new COVID variant.

If something doesn't feel right, listen to that reluctant voice in your head telling you not to proceed. Polling coworkers to get the desired answer will get you in trouble. There's always an idiot willing to agree with you. Everyone wants validation when entering a gray area. Someone to blame when the brilliant idea turns to shit. If you need to ask if something is legal, chances are, it's not.

HOW WILL THEY KNOW?

The hiring process to become a New York City police officer can take several years. Before handing you a gun and shield, the department wants to get to know you. Besides a thorough background check, police recruits must endure physical and psychological exams. If the department discovers you misled or withheld important facts from your past, they will fire you on the spot.

Early in my NYPD career one of my childhood friends was considering a career change. He began picking my brain about the NYPD's hiring process. After answering his questions, I had a few of my own.

"Didn't you have a suspended driver's license?"

"Yeah, but that's in California and Virginia," he replied.

My friend was a military brat who piled up moving violations in several states during his teenage years. The running joke was he couldn't drive in half the states in the country.

"You have to get that cleaned up before you can be a police officer," I explained.

"How are they even going to know?" he asked.

"What do you think this is, 1972? Everything is computerized," I laughed.

"You think they would check?" he said.

"This isn't McDonald's. It's the New York City Police Department. Of course they're going to check."

I had to explain to my naïve friend that his driving record was easily attainable.

"If you don't get that cleared up, they're never going to hire you."

"Boy, I'm glad I paid the fines on my New York State driver's license," he replied.

"Your license was suspended in New York, too?"

"Yeah, don't worry, I took care of it."

"I'm not worried about it. But you should be," I replied.

"My license was suspended so many times that there was a note attached to my driving record that read, see archives," he laughed.

My friend didn't grasp that the New York City Police Department wasn't interested in hiring racecar drivers. But that didn't stop him from taking the next police exam. A few months later, he called to complain that his investigator from the police applicant division was giving him a hard time.

"This guy is busting my balls about my driving record," he fumed.

"I told you he would."

"I should have never listened to you."

"What are you talking about?"

"I took your advice and told my police investigator about my driving record. Now he's on my ass," my friend complained.

"He would have found out eventually."

"No fucking way," he snapped.

What could I say? Nothing seemed to sink into my friend's thick head. A few weeks later, he received a rejection letter, ending his NYPD career before it began.

It was for the best. The NYPD is an unforgiving employer for those who don't follow the rules. Even if he had been hired, his temper would have gotten the better of him at some point.

My father knew my friend since he was a child and was curious why he hadn't started the police academy. When I explained what happened, my father replied, "That's okay. The world needs guys to unclog toilets too."

COULD YOU DO ME A FAVOR?

When his driving record cost him a career in law enforcement, my friend got a job working for a small town in Upstate New York. The hulking plumber spent his day snaking drains for the sewer department.

On call twenty-four-seven, he carried a beeper the size of a deck of cards that went off at the most inopportune times.

Obstructed catch basins interrupted Thanksgiving dinners and fantasy football drafts.

"You have to leave?" I asked after his pager went off during the Super Bowl.

"They're making it worth my while." He'd laughed at the overtime earned for responding to emergencies.

As much as he enjoyed the job, he often complained about his coworkers.

"All these guys have to do is unclog a few drains, and they're never around."

"What do you mean?" I asked.

"All of them have side gigs that are more important than their day job."

"I guess they're not pulling their weight?"

"They're either coming in late, leaving early, or disappearing for half the day," he groused.

One evening, over a couple of drinks, I could tell something was on my childhood friend's mind.

"I have a question for you," he asked.

"Yeah?" I replied.

This wasn't the first time my rough-and-tumble friend asked that question. Prone to making questionable decisions, he would often solicit my advice after the damage was done.

"Something happened at work," he mumbled.

"And?"

"I need your legal advice," he whispered.

"Is this something you're contemplating? Or did it already happen?" I asked.

"Oh, it already happened," he groaned.

My civilian friends were blue-collar guys who didn't engage in criminal activity. As much as I wanted to hear what was troubling him, I wouldn't risk my police career. Before he said another word, I had to explain the ground rules.

"Listen, Frankie, if you're going to tell me about a crime, you understand I have to report it," I explained.

"I know," he replied, ordering another round of drinks and telling his story.

One morning, he and a coworker were repairing a pumping station on the outskirts of town. While they were finishing up, the coworker received a cryptic call. The man spoke in hushed tones and began scribbling in his notepad while assuring the caller "he would take care of it."

"Sounds clandestine," I laughed.

"He hangs up the phone and asks if I wouldn't mind doing him a favor," my friend said.

Having known my buddy my entire life, I could tell whatever happened had shaken him.

"We drive to a rough part of town and park behind a beat-up two-story house. There are all these people out front directing us into the house. We climb a flight of stairs and go into a bedroom where a dead guy is lying in a bed," my friend explained.

"Don't you work for the sewer department?" I asked.

"Yeah, but unbeknownst to me, my coworker works part time for a ghetto funeral home in South Jersey."

"Why would he take you to see a DOA?" I asked.

"He tells me to go down to the truck and grab a body bag he keeps stashed in his toolbox. When I return, there's a minister in this tiny bedroom reading from the Bible. After he's done blessing the stiff, we put him in the body bag and carry him downstairs. Our work van is filled with tools and equipment. So, to make room for the body, we had to move things around in the back of the truck."

"What did you do with the dead guy while rearranging the truck?"

"We had to lay him down in the vacant lot," my friend explained.

As disturbing as the story was, it was comical. A pair of sewer workers transporting a deceased man to a funeral home in a plumbing truck.

"This sounds like an episode from *The Sopranos*," I laughed.

"Don't laugh. It gets worse," my friend said, polishing off his beer.

"How can carrying a body down a flight of stairs into a work van get any worse?"

"I asked my coworker where we were going. He assured me it was not far. The next thing I know, we're heading south on the Garden State Parkway with a dead man rolling around in the back of the truck. It felt like we were driving forever before we got off at Asbury Park," my friend elaborated.

"Asbury Park? That's seventy miles from where you work."

"Tell me about it. The name of the town is written all over the work van. All somebody had to do was call city hall and report us."

"What happened when you got to the funeral home?" I asked.

"We pull around the back of the building, and my coworker gets out and starts banging on the rear door. This scary-looking guy in a lab coat comes out and tells us to bring the body inside. We carry him in and place him on a metal slab next to an embalming machine. My God, the smell in that place was awful."

"Did he at least pay you after putting you through all that?" I asked.

"On the ride back, I'm steaming. I'm trying to keep calm and not strangle this guy when he reaches into his pocket, hands me a fifty-dollar bill, and says, 'Thanks for giving me a hand.' Give you a hand? We just moved a dead body across state lines."

"That was nice of him," I laughed.

"Then, he has the balls to tell me there's more where that came from."

"Are you kidding me?"

"I wish I was. I told him the funeral home would embalm two bodies if he ever did that to me again," my friend replied.

My buddy was a plumber working for a small town tasked with clearing sewer lines. He didn't sign up for *Weekend at Bernie's*. After listening to this bizarre story, one question remained.

"So, Vic, let me ask you, is that legal?" my friend asked.

"No comment," I replied.

QUALITY CONTROL

The New York City Police Department is like *The Firm*. An organization obsessed with monitoring its employees. Every January, NYPD members are required to meet with their integrity control officer for a quasi-background check. There is no appointment or advanced notice. One day after roll call, you'll get summoned to the ICO's office.

After taking a seat, the paunchy bureaucrat asks for your driver's license and vehicle registration. You try to make small talk, but he ignores you. He's too busy staring into his computer terminal, searching for suspensions and unpaid parking tickets. When he's done, Wilford Brimley returns the documents and asks to see your firearms. The department wants to ensure you haven't lost a gun and forgot to tell them about it. After checking all the boxes, your ICO becomes chatty.

"How is everything going?" he asked with the sincerity of a used car salesman.

"Great," I replied.

"Is there anything going on in the precinct I should know about?" he quizzed.

"The vending machines are out of M&M's," I mocked.

"Look, Vic. My job is to root out corruption at the precinct level. If you're aware of police corruption and don't report it, it will fall on you," the middle-aged lieutenant warned.

ICOs are like a box of chocolates. You never know what you'll get when the department deputizes middle management to micromanage.

Most integrity control officers like to stay behind the scenes. Hiding in the shadows, they make their presence known when necessary. Others are bulls in a china shop who get involved in things that aren't in their job description. They'll hound cops running the precinct club demanding to see the books, hoping to catch them skimming money from raffle tickets or the vending machines in the station house lobby.

Trust me, no one ever got rich running the precinct club.

Some ICOs will caution local restaurants not to offer discounted meals to police officers. God forbid anyone get a free cup of coffee.

Most integrity control officers are spineless company men posing as homicide detectives. If they had investigative skills, they'd lead a detective squad, not search for unpaid parking tickets.

My ICO wouldn't unearth police corruption by asking ridiculous questions. If I knew about police corruption, the last person I'd share it with would be him.

NYPD protocol mandates its members to report police corruption immediately. For me to answer meant I was holding something back, which would result in my suspension. It was obvious he wasn't looking to do me any favors. If I had information about police corruption, I would call the Internal Affairs Bureau.

Pretending to be hurt by my lack of trust, the disingenuous lieutenant removed his glasses from his large melon and said, "Vic, you can always come to me if something doesn't look right. Think of me as a Dutch uncle."

Uncle? Is this guy kidding me?

Growing up, I had three loving uncles. None of them tried to fuck me over like this guy. The oily ICO didn't want to get blindsided by an Internal Affairs Investigation. Playing liar's poker with every cop in the precinct, he figured he might unearth something he could run to IAB with and look like a hero.

I saw through his childish head game and responded with sarcastic answers. The only thing he got out of me that day were complaints about the snacks in the vending machines.

A MAN WITHOUT A COUNTRY

Your right to privacy ends when you become a member of the New York City Police Department. The department saves every form you fill out in case they have to use it against you later.

Working under the umbrella of the Organized Crime Control Bureau (OCCB) is worse. Every year, OCCB members complete a lengthy survey. Marital status, children's names, and major purchases are shared with the department. As intrusive as it sounds, there is a good reason for it. The NYPD tries to prevent space cadets from reaching units where sensitive information is handled.

One free-spirited detective I knew lived a bohemian lifestyle and refused to be moored by conventional living arrangements.

The guy was a nomad, moving from one place to another at a moment's notice. When you'd ask where he lived, the cagey detective was vague, only naming the borough. I'd often tease him about what living in the Witness Protection Program was like, which prohibits its members from revealing personal information. He worked in my office for ten years, and the only time he revealed anything from his past was when he mentioned being a standout pitcher in high school.

According to him, he could throw in the mid-nineties and was scouted by several major league baseball teams.

I had no reason to doubt his claim because he could throw a football almost a hundred yards in his mid-forties.

"Why didn't you go pro?" I asked.

"I got sidetracked," he replied.

"Who are you? Roy Hobbs?" I laughed.

One night, while spending the night with his sister in a Queens housing project, the transient detective couldn't find a parking space. Instead of circling the block, Roy Hobbs parked his vehicle in the building's restricted parking lot.

He tossed his NYPD parking permit on the dashboard, hoping it would prevent him from receiving a parking ticket.

Several residents noticed the brightly colored placard and complained to the Internal Affairs Bureau. They questioned how an NYPD member making over sixty thousand dollars a year could live in a low-income housing unit. Realizing he had opened a can of worms, Roy Hobbs turned to our lieutenant for help.

"All right, I'll straighten this out, but you have to find a permanent residence immediately," the lieutenant instructed.

Roy Hobbs thanked the lieutenant and assured him he'd find an apartment by the end of the week.

When the Internal Affairs Bureau contacted our lieutenant, he explained his detective was visiting his sister on the night in question and didn't live in the housing projects.

The Internal Affairs Bureau supervisor then asked for the detective's address, prompting our lieutenant to cup his hand over the phone's mouthpiece and shout across the office to his homeless detective, "Hey Nicky, where are you living now?" he asked.

Stunned by the question, Roy Hobbs dug through his Rolodex for a phone number. Annoyed by his lack of a response, the lieutenant yelled, "Nicky, I need an address for IAB."

"Lou, can I get back to you with that?" the detective replied while frantically dialing numbers on his desk phone.

The look on the lieutenant's face was priceless as he attempted to stall the Internal Affairs Bureau while his nitwit detective called family members for an address.

"I gave him a month to find a permanent residence. How does he not know where he lives?" the astonished lieutenant asked.

"Maybe he got sidetracked," I kidded.

"Sidetracked? This fucking guy really is Roy Hobbs. Nobody knows a damn thing about him," my lieutenant griped.

The NYPD insists on stability and frowns upon its members living a fugitive lifestyle, moving from one residence to another.

THAT'S NEWS TO ME

A friend of mine had a close encounter with disaster when his integrity control officer called him into his office.

"I have to show you something," the lieutenant said, holding a computer printout of his driver's license.

After seventeen years with the New York City Police Department, the Bronx sergeant feared this day would come.

As a New Jersey teenager, he was hell on wheels, racking up moving violations before joining the NYPD. When he went to pay his fines at the New Jersey Department of Motor Vehicles, the shady clerk told him it would be less expensive if he updated his driver's license and omitted his middle initial.

"Is that legal?" he asked.

"Sure," the clerk said, handing him the paperwork.

It sounded fugazy. But who was he to argue with a New Jersey Department of Motor Vehicles employee?

He completed the driver's license renewal form and dropped his middle name. Fifteen minutes later, he was a new man with a new identity. He never gave the forged document a second thought until his ICO approached him about the matter seventeen years later.

"Bobby, I think you have a suspended driver's license," the ICO said.

"Lieutenant?" he asked, feigning surprise.

"It looks like you've had a suspended driver's license since 1990," the lieutenant said, handing him the computerized printout.

The sergeant had to think of something fast before his world came crashing down. Termination, suspension, and the loss of vacation days were all variable options.

"Lieutenant, that's not me. I don't use my middle initial," the sergeant said, producing his driver's license.

The lieutenant stared at the driver's license for several seconds before returning it to the sergeant.

"What are the odds of that? Two guys from Bradley Beach with the same name and date of birth," the lieutenant said before making a notation on the printout and walking away.

When my friend told me the story, I said, "I'm shocked he didn't ask for your middle name."

"Vic, he's the ICO, not a detective," my friend laughed.

THE RED MENACE

New York City began installing red light cameras across its five boroughs in the early nineties. Under the guise of public safety, the program was implemented to prevent vehicle accidents. Red light cameras are a scam that generates millions of dollars in revenue for a city that nickel and dimes its residents.

Snapping the photo of a license plate passing through a red light doesn't prevent traffic accidents. If anything, it creates them when motorists are rear-ended for slamming on their brakes to avoid a red light summons.

No one asked New Yorkers if they wanted city hall to have another way to pick their pockets. Like dandelions, the red menace began popping up across the city. The Orwellian cameras sparked outrage in Queens and Staten Island when residents began receiving traffic tickets in the mail. Spray paint, gunfire, and a stick of dynamite were used to exact revenge against the red light cameras.

At the time, I had an apartment in my aunt's building down the block from my parent's house. The mailman often confused my father with me because we shared the same name. I often got my father's bills and junk mail while he glommed my health magazines.

There are no advantages to your father reading your mail. I felt thirteen years old as my old man rummaged through my things while commenting on my reading material.

"Hey, jerkoff. Did you get my AAA renewal?" my father asked.

"Do you have my *Men's Health* magazine?" I replied.

"Yeah," my father laughed.

"What's so funny?" I asked.

"*Men's Health*? What a crock of shit. Give me eight dollars a month, and I'll tell you what's healthy," my father replied.

One night, I stopped by my parent's house to pick up my mail when I got ambushed by Jack Ruby waving a piece of paper.

"Hey, Johnny Law. Just because you're a cop doesn't give you the right to blow through red lights," my father laughed.

"I didn't go through a red light. What are you talking about?"

"Rosedale Avenue and the Cross Bronx Expressway ring a bell?"

"Dad, I didn't go through a red light."

"Sure you did. It's right here," my father said, flicking the paper into my chest.

I examined the form and laughed. It was a red light summons mailed to the registered owner of a 1990 Dodge Shadow. On the front was a grainy black-and-white still photo of my father's car passing through a red light.

"Laugh, but that red light just cost you fifty dollars," my father said.

"It won't cost me anything. That's your car."

My father looked like I had informed him of the passing of a relative. He snatched the paper from my hand and threw on his readers for a better look.

"How the fuck can this be? I don't drive through red lights," my father shouted.

"Well, that's your car. The red menace got you," I replied.

"Can you take care of this for me?" my father asked.

My father believed I could move heaven and earth as a member of the New York Police Department. Whenever he got a parking ticket or a sanitation summons for placing recyclables in the trash, he'd call me to complain.

"Dad, I can't squash this. It's from the Department of Traffic."

"Motherfuckers. I'll bet it's a faulty camera," my father groaned.

"You can't fight city hall."

"The fuck I can't. I'm going to fight this in court."

"Good luck with that."

"Vic, can they do this?" my father asked, pointing to the letter.

"They already did," I replied.

"I mean, is this legal?" my father asked.

CHAPTER 4

YOU CAN NEVER BE
TOO PREPARED FOR DEATH

I was thirteen years old when my mother started preparing me for death. "Listen, your father and I will not be around forever," she said as we sat down to dinner.

"What's that supposed to mean?" I asked.

My late mother had the organizational skills of a German banker and believed in doing something sooner rather than later. Before I could walk, I had a social security number. She dragged me to the Department of Labor on my fourteenth birthday to get working papers. My parents were in their late thirties and in excellent health. I couldn't conceive what life would be without them.

"Well, your father and I are eventually going to die, and you'll have to handle our arrangements," my mother explained.

"Arrangements? What has to be arranged?" I asked.

"I want to be cremated," my mother said.

Where was this coming from? I just wanted to finish dinner and go outside and play with my friends. I didn't sign up for a funeral director's course.

After instructing me on what size urn to purchase, my mother turned to my father and asked, "Victor, is there anything you'd like to add?"

The only thing my father wanted was another meatball on his plate. Putting down his fork, my father took a deep breath and said, "The only thing fair about life is death."

"What do you mean?" I asked.

I could tell by the look on my mother's face that wasn't what she wanted to hear. "That's not what I meant," she interrupted.

"Victor, we're all going to die. It doesn't matter how rich or poor you are because we're all headed to the same place," my father explained.

"Saint Raymond's Cemetery?" I asked.

"Victor, you're confusing him," my mother shouted.

"Jesus Christ, Maryann, I don't care. Put me out with the trash on Thursday night," my father snapped.

Although he was teasing, there was a lot of truth to my father's statement. My dad was a no-frills kind of guy and didn't see the point in worrying about something he had no control over.

"Victor, don't be silly," my mother replied.

"Maryann, I don't care if you put me in a Hefty bag," my father said, twirling the spaghetti on his plate.

"How can you say that?" my mother asked.

"What do I care what happens to me after I'm dead? That's going to be someone else's problem," my father laughed.

My old man's comments had lightened the mood. But the bizarre conversation exposed the differences in philosophies my parents had on the subject.

My father didn't care what happened to his remains after his death, while my mother prepared for the end like an Egyptian pharaoh. None of this made sense to me. Funerals and flower arrangements were thirty years down the road. At thirteen, I couldn't purchase a casket or tour a crematorium.

"Mom, why are you telling me this?" I asked.

"Because you can never be too prepared for death," she explained.

Some thirty years later, it would all make sense. But at the time, I thought my mother had lost her mind. As far as I knew, everyone in my family had a way to go before worrying about death.

MR. VAN BUREN

My brother and I chose different paths for our NYPD careers. I racked up hundreds of arrests and was promoted to detective. Fredo spent his days subverting police work, holed up in a spider hole behind the boiler room of a Manhattan precinct. He amassed eight arrests during his uneventful career, telling anyone who'd listen, including his father, how hard he worked.

"They're working your brother to death," my father complained.

"Dad, Fredo has a clerical position," I laughed.

"Yeah, but he's responsible for all that property," my father replied.

"Dad, Fredo works ten hours a week. The rest of the time, he's searching for the nearest deli," I said.

A few months after graduating from the police academy, Fredo became disillusioned with police work and applied for the property clerk position. A property clerk is responsible for the storage of property that enters the station house. Everything from arrest evidence to found property is stored in a metal locker behind the front desk. A precinct property locker can house anything from narcotics to a found wallet.

Every few days, the locker fills with an assortment of crap, prompting Fredo to get off his ass and load a police van with the property. From there, he delivers its contents to the property clerk's office in Lower Manhattan. Since he started his days at the crack of dawn, Fredo was done by noon.

The early hours gave my carnivorous brother ample time to pursue his passion for cured meats. My younger sibling has the diet of a gluttonous Roman and would forgo an orgy for a six-inch reuben. If you think I'm kidding, I'm not, and it's not pretty. I've watched him devour swatches of red meat drenched in Russian dressing oozing between his stubby fingers like it was his last meal.

"This is better than sex," Fredo said as I picked at my turkey club.

"Don't you worry about cholesterol?"

"Cholesterol? Grandma and Grandpa ate like shit and lived into their eighties."

"Yeah, and they both developed Alzheimer's disease."

"Listen, as long as I can get a sandwich like this, I don't care if I lose my mind," Fredo mocked while licking the grease off his fingers.

"Keep eating like that, and you're going to get the runs."

"I already have the runs," Fredo laughed.

"Then why do you keep shoveling that shit into your face?"

"Just because you have the shits doesn't mean you have to deprive the rest of your body of vital nutrients," Fredo explained while sliding a kosher pickle down his throat.

I learned a long time ago not to debate my philosophical brother. Fredo lives in his own universe, void of responsibility and common sense.

Unlike my brother, I took my NYPD career seriously, working long hours and holidays while he rarely left the station house. On the rare occasions he did, it was to run an errand.

Anybody who meets my brother thinks he's the greatest thing since sliced bread. Fredo is a schmoozer and tells everyone what they want to hear. Unfortunately, I'm fact-driven and tell it like it is. I realize I sound like Ferris Bueller's jealous sister complaining about my brother getting away with murder. But it's my story to tell. If Fredo wants to explain where he spent his days during his NYPD career, he can write his own book.

While inspecting the precinct property locker one morning, Fredo noticed a foot-long square box on a shelf. Printed on the top of the dusty box was the name Calhoun Van Buren, 1925-1959.

"One box of cremated ashes? What the fuck is this?" Fredo said, reading the property voucher while shaking the old gray box up and down. Inside, fragmented pieces of bone danced like a damaged USPS parcel.

Jesus, they did a half-assed job cremating this guy, Fredo thought, moving the box closer to his ear.

Realizing this could be a problem, Fredo hunted down the rookie cop who vouchered the box of charred remains.

"Is this some kind of joke?" Fredo asked, waving the box of ashes in the young cop's face.

"I found it under a dead woman's bed," the rookie explained.

"So why didn't you leave it there?"

"My training sergeant told me to voucher it for safekeeping."

"Safekeeping? It's a box of fucking ashes!" Fredo snapped.

"Well, my sergeant ordered me," the rookie reiterated.

"What's the value of a box of ashes?" Fredo shouted, shoving the box into the rookie cop's hands.

In all fairness, it wasn't the rookie's fault. In field training, you do as you're told. The late Mrs. Van Buren lived alone in the sparsely furnished apartment before passing in her bed. The elderly widow had left no instructions on what to do with her late husband's remains.

The training sergeant figured it would be good for the rookie cop to learn how to handle decedents property. Unfortunately for my brother, he inherited a headache.

"I don't know if they'll accept this at the property clerk's office," Fredo stated before walking away from the confused rookie. A few days later, when the property locker was full, Fredo loaded a precinct van with miscellaneous crap for the ride to the property clerk's office in Lower Manhattan.

"Listen, I'm going to try to sneak that box of ashes in. So keep your mouth shut," Fredo warned his lackey, Barry.

"Why would I say anything?" Barry asked.

"Because you have a big mouth," Fredo replied.

Barry's mouth ran like a leaky faucet. And despite this, Fredo kept him around because he served a purpose. My brother would make an excellent cult leader. He has a gift for attracting morons to do his bidding.

Fredo found the perfect flunky in the low-voltage Barry. Before joining the NYPD, Barry was a federal investigator for the United States Department of Agriculture, or USDA. Try as he might, the pork chop cop wasn't suited for the mean streets of New York City. Barry thought of Fredo as a mentor and would take a bullet for my duplicitous brother, provided a crazed gunman found his way into the precinct basement.

The pork chop cop's wife was equally simple and believed she could predict aviation disasters.

Fredo stashed the box containing the late Calhoun Van Buren in the back of a large wooden push dolly filled with property, hoping it wouldn't get noticed at the property clerk's storage facility.

"What's this?" the clerk asked, examining the box of ashes.

"It's a box of cremated ashes," Fredo replied.

Like a scale, the clerk balanced the decrepit box in his hand. While debating what to do, the pork chop cop weighed in. "I get the creeps looking at that box," he said.

Spooked, the clerk quickly put the box on the counter like it contained uranium. "We can't accept this," he said.

"Why not?" Fredo asked.

"We don't store human remains here," the clerk said.

"It's not human remains. It's ashes," Fredo argued.

"Sorry, but I can't accept this," the clerk said, thumbing through a stack of property invoices.

"So, what am I supposed to do with them?"

"That's not my problem. You're going to have to find a relative to take this off your hands," the clerk said before walking away from the counter.

Annoyed, Fredo said nothing until he and big-mouth Barry reached the parking lot.

"Why did you open your mouth?" Fredo shouted.

"Well, I do get the creeps looking at the box," Barry replied.

"You didn't have to tell the clerk that."

"My wife thinks Mr. Van Buren died of a heart attack."

"Barry, please shut the fuck up about your psychic wife until I figure out what to do with this box of ashes," Fredo shouted.

As angry as Fredo was, it wouldn't prevent him from working on a heart attack. It was almost lunchtime, which meant visiting New York City's premiere delicatessen. A sandwich from Katz's Deli was just what the cardiologist ordered. Established in 1888, Katz's Kosher Deli is a New York City landmark famous for its delicious sandwiches.

With blood sugar levels falling, Fredo grabbed a parking spot around the corner from the Lower East Side deli. As they exited the property van, a radio car from the Seventh Precinct rolled up.

"I hope you have nothing of value in that van," the precinct cop said.

"What are you talking about?" Fredo asked.

"They break into a lot of vehicles on this block," the cop warned.

"Nope, it's empty," Fredo replied.

Fredo thanked the cop for the heads up before making a beeline for Katz's Deli.

"Hey, Fredo, aren't you forgetting something?" Barry asked.

"What are you talking about?" Fredo replied.

"The box of ashes," Barry said.

"Are you fucking kidding me?" Fredo snapped.

"What happens if somebody breaks into the van and steals it?" Barry explained.

Babbling Barry had a point. The box of ashes had a voucher number. At some point, somebody would be looking for it. Fredo would face department charges if the box were lost or stolen.

"Yeah, you're right," Fredo replied, walking back to the van to retrieve the box from under the front seat.

Minutes later, Fredo and his disciple were gorging themselves on hot pastrami in a corner booth of Katz's Deli.

"Oh my God," Fredo said, savoring the last bite of his three-thousand-calorie sandwich.

"It's terrible, isn't it?" the pork chop cop said.

"What the fuck are you talking about? This is the best sandwich in the city," Fredo replied.

"I mean Mr. Van Buren."

"Who?"

"Mr. Van Buren," Barry pointed to the box of ashes on the table.

"Barry, if you're so concerned about Mr. Van Buren, why don't you take him home?"

"I can't do that. My wife would get attached to his energy."

When she wasn't predicting the next plane crash, the pork chop cop's wife believed she could communicate with the dead.

"Barry, if you don't mind, let me finish my sandwich in peace?"

"Fredo, you did the right thing by not leaving him in the van."

"You're right. God forbid, I lose this." Fredo mocked, patting the box with his fingers.

"Something like that could keep you out of heaven."

"Heaven?"

"Fredo, if you were to lose Mr. Van Buren's ashes, God would judge you," Barry explained.

Fredo knew his partner was a moron. That was why he kept him around. Fredo needed someone to handle the grunt work while he napped or vanished to run errands on department time.

"Barry, I don't want to wind up in the trial room (NYPD disciplinary court). I'm not worried about going to hell."

"Well, you should," the Pentecostal pinhead replied.

"Barry, could you please shut the fuck up?" Fredo growled.

When they returned to the precinct, Fredo handed Barry the box of ashes.

"He's your responsibility now," Fredo fumed.

For the next six months, Fredo tried every trick in the book to rid himself of the late Calhoun Van Buren while Barry took him everywhere he went.

Monday to Friday, Mr. Van Buren's ashes toured the city in the property van while spending his weekends in Barry's living room on Long Island.

"Barry, why don't you just leave that in your locker?" Fredo gestured to the well-traveled parcel of human remains.

"Fredo, I wouldn't be able to live with myself if something happened to this box," Barry replied.

Fredo had a problem. He couldn't hold on to Mr. Van Buren forever or toss him in the trash. A family member or city agency was needed to provide disposition documents for the precinct property ledger.

After months of finagling, Fredo discovered the answer to his problem lay on a forgotten Island. Hart's Island rests in the cold waters of the Long Island Sound between the Bronx and the north shore of Long Island. The nondescript one-mile patch of land is rich in history, once serving as a Confederate prison camp during the Civil War. Hart's Island also housed missile silos during the cold war era. Today, the barren peninsula is used to bury New York City's unclaimed dead.

Several times a week, a ferry carries a work detail of Rikers Island inmates and pine boxes across the Long Island Sound to Hart's Island.

The cheap coffins contain those with no means of a proper burial. The unclaimed dead are buried in unmarked graves in a potter's field. There are no last words or grieving relatives to commemorate their lives. For the price of two Rangers tickets, Fredo secured a cemetery plot for the late Calhoun Van Buren.

On a cold February morning, a ferry's foghorn pushed through the morning air on its approach to City Island. Waiting on the restricted dock were two men and a box of ashes.

Cradling the box in the crook of his arm, Barry asked, "Fredo, are they going to let us ride out to the island?"

"Barry, why would you want to go to that godforsaken place?"

"Well, I think we should say a few words before he's buried."

"Barry, you didn't know the guy. Give it a rest."

While the old diesel ferry maneuvered alongside the rickety dock, a Department of Corrections van filled with inmates rolled into the parking lot.

"They're here," Fredo said.

As Fredo made his way to the cargo van, Barry reluctantly followed a few paces behind.

"Paul, I appreciate you helping me with this," Fredo said, handing the correction officer an envelope through the open van window.

"No problem," the portly jail guard replied, opening the envelope to examine the hockey tickets.

Clutching the box under his arm, Barry asked: "Will he have his own grave?

"Is he kidding?" the correction officer asked.

There was a level of risk with the impromptu funeral. The backroom deal hadn't been approved through the proper channels. There could be consequences for tossing Mr. Van Buren into an unmarked grave.

"He's pulling your leg," Fredo replied to the nervous corrections officer.

"Shouldn't we at least say a few words?" Barry asked.

"A few words? Are you out of your mind? Give him the box," Fredo barked.

"Look, Fredo, I'd love to help you out, but I don't have time for this," the correction officer replied.

Fredo couldn't believe his ears. Seconds away from unloading the albatross of ashes, his flunky decides to ask questions. Fredo was stuck with the box if the correction officer got cold feet.

"Barry, whatever emotional attachment you have to that thing, you had better get over it," Fredo said.

Reluctantly, Barry did what he was told and handed over the remains of the late Calhoun Van Buren. He looked like he wanted to cry when the ferry filled with grave diggers set sail for Hart's Island to bury his new friend.

"Well, now that it's settled, let's get something to eat," Fredo said, rubbing his stomach.

"Fredo, can we just go back to the precinct?" Barry sighed.

"Listen, Barry, I'm sorry for your loss, but that's not happening." My brother is not a sentimental guy. He's governed by a gluttonous appetite that waits for no man. I've watched him pull his car to the side of the road and tear into a hot pizza meant for his waiting family.

"But, Fredo, I'm not hungry," Barry said.

"Barry, I realize you're in mourning. But I'm getting a knish and a cream soda from Katz's Deli," Fredo replied.

"Fredo, I don't think you understand. We did a terrible thing."

"Barry, get in the van, or I'm leaving you here."

Later, at Katz's Deli, Barry attempted to get Fredo to atone for his sins.

"Fredo, do you ever worry about karma?" Barry asked.

"Barry, twenty minutes after I finish this knish, I'm going to have the shits."

"So?" Barry asked.

"That's karma," Fredo explained.

The ordeal haunted Barry, while Fredo never gave it a second thought. Ironically, Mr. Van Buren was buried in the same potter's field as his wife when no one claimed her remains from the city morgue.

Despite her decades of planning, my mother's passing left plenty of unfinished business. As unpleasant as it was, I did my best to honor her wishes. A lot can happen over thirty years, leaving wills and funeral arrangements obsolete. My mother was consumed with death, while my father never gave it a second thought. Ironically, they both ended up in the same place, resting peacefully in an antique cabinet in my living room.

CHAPTER 5

YOUNG & STUPID

Teenagers think they're invincible. Money, health, and legal woes are someone else's problems when you're young and stupid. That won't happen to me. They'll laugh when warned of life's perils. One advantage to aging is the wisdom you'll gather along the highway of life.

While traveling this path, you see countless examples of poor decisions that have ruined many lives. We get a clean slate out of the womb before life's temptations knock. Then, it's up to you to head home before the trouble starts.

Life is a game of inches, and if your ass is hanging out of bounds, it can cost you dearly. Unfortunately, most teenagers are oblivious to this and find out once it's too late.

"One bad decision can ruin your life," my father would lecture during my formidable years. Having had several close calls with the law, my father wasn't about to let his son make the same mistakes.

Sadly, there is no warning light to alert teenagers to impending danger. Once they've crossed that line, they have to deal with the consequences. As a rambunctious teen, I came close to crossing that line many times. Years later, when I became a member of the NYPD, I tried to keep that in mind when I came across teenagers who straddled that sometimes indistinguishable line.

"IT'S IN GOD'S HANDS"

Many radio car partnerships are marriages of convenience. Most precinct cops despise walking a foot post or guarding a hospitalized prisoner, so they'll work with the village idiot. Jumping into a police car with a lazy cop can be frustrating and sometimes dangerous. During my NYPD career, I was selective about who I worked with. However, there were plenty of times I had no say in the matter. Sometimes, it's a shotgun wedding for the evening when your partner calls in sick.

One awful marriage I had to endure was the night I got stuck working with the laziest cop in the precinct. You could hear the laughter of the outgoing platoon when our names got read aloud together at roll call.

"Sarge, please don't make me work with this guy," I begged.

"Sorry, Vic. Your partner's not here, and nobody else wants to work with him," the patrol sergeant replied.

Shit Can Sammy was a fat, swarthy slob in a police uniform. His beady eyes hid beneath a mop of unkempt hair flanked by a thick unibrow. The fifteen-year veteran looked like an out-of-shape mall cop with a collage of food stains on his uniform shirt.

Known for squashing radio runs in seconds, Shit Can Sammy would race past locations at forty miles an hour before marking the job 90x (unfounded) without stepping out of his radio car to investigate.

The Sultan of Sluggish once responded three times to the same building after residents complained of a foul odor from an elderly tenant's apartment. While Granny decomposed, Shit Can Sammy gave her neighbors the runaround. He explained the stench coming from Grandma's apartment was probably garlic. After a while, the tenants had enough of the rank smell and broke down the door to find the dead woman rotting in her bed.

When asked why he didn't attempt to gain entry to the apartment, Shit Can Sammy explained he had lost his sense of smell and couldn't detect the putrid smell of death. As punishment, the lazy patrolman got dumped into the precinct school unit. He was expected to handle whatever problems arose at the local middle school. Within days, a panicked school crossing guard ran up to Shit Can Sammy's radio car after a gang of thugs had robbed her. Annoyed, the plump patrolman began wrapping up the half-eaten Italian combo in his lap as the crossing guard pointed to the fleeing teens.

"Can I eat in peace?" he shouted before driving away from the startled woman.

I didn't want to work with the lazy piece of shit. But I had no choice. So, I dutifully complied. After roll call, the troll-like creature pulled me to the side to set the tone for the evening.

"Hey, Ferrari, you're not looking for a collar tonight?" he asked.

Before I could answer, the fat whiner gave me a list of excuses why he couldn't get involved with an arrest.

"Vic, my back is killing me, and I have plans tomorrow. I can't work late tonight, you understand?" he explained.

I wasn't the first to hear this song and dance. Every cop in the precinct got the same bullshit story when they got stuck working with Shit Can Sammy.

After dragging his fat ass into the radio car, he reminisced about his long and undistinguished NYPD career.

One bullshit story after another rolled out of his mouth while conveniently omitting his shortcomings as a cop. Pulling the seniority card, Shit Can Sammy insisted on driving to steer us away from anything that would lead to an arrest. As we drove around the quiet part of the precinct, he rambled on while I monitored the radio for calls in our sector.

"I used to be like you," he said.

"Thin?" I replied.

"I was an active cop too. One year, I made over a hundred arrests," Shit Can Sammy boasted.

I may have had three years on the job, but it was obvious this clown never took his handcuffs out of his case.

The one thing you can't do is bullshit another cop. There are no secrets in the New York City Police Department. Before you step inside the precinct, every cop knows your act. Rats, headhunters, poachers, drunks, and empty suits are all preceded by their reputations. It's tough to fool trained observers watching your every move. I tuned Shit Can Sammy out when he started with the imaginary war stories.

I tried my best to get through the evening with a lazy malcontent who had an excuse every time I attempted to pick up a job.

"That's not in our sector," or "That's a bullshit call," he'd utter when I reached for the radio.

With our shift ending in minutes, I answered a radio run of teenagers throwing bottles off the roof of a building.

"What the fuck are you doing?" Shit Can Sammy barked.

"The job is two blocks from the precinct," I replied.

"So?" he complained.

Before picking up the late-night call, Shit Can Sammy had lived up to his reputation. He rolled his eyes every time he had to fill out a report or exit the car for a traffic stop.

The building didn't have an elevator, which meant the stairs, as the out-of-shape cop continued to bitch.

"Now I have to fucking climb stairs," Shit Can Sammy moaned.

When we reached the roof, I turned down my radio, took out my flashlight, and opened the heavy steel door. I walked across the asphalt roof, shining my flashlight into the darkness of the night.

Shit Can Sammy was ready to call it a night five seconds later.

"See, I told you this was bullshit," he said before turning around and heading toward the stairwell.

At the other end of the roof, I spotted a few empty beer bottles and a pile of clothing rolled up in a ball. "Hold on, Sammy," I said, walking over to investigate.

As I approached, I could hear a faint moan. Shining my flashlight on the pile of clothes, I realized it was a young boy rolled up in the fetal position.

"Are you okay?" I asked, pointing my flashlight into the unresponsive teen's glassy eyes.

Grabbing his shoulder to prop him up, I got hit with the stench of vomit.

"Hey, wake up!" I shouted into the boy's face.

The young man was anything but okay. He was dying from hypothermia and alcohol poisoning.

"Central, we have an overdose on the roof of 633 West 234th Street. Put a rush on the bus," I shouted into my radio.

By the looks of things, it must have been quite a party. The roof had enough empty beer bottles to put several grown men on their backs. After passing out from overindulging, his friends abandoned him to fend for himself. Between the alcohol and frigid temperature, it was a wonder the drunken teenager was still alive.

While I tended to the unconscious boy, Shit Can Sammy had a meltdown.

"You had to pick up this fucking job," he griped.

"Shut the fuck up, asshole!" I shouted back.

The kid barely had a pulse, and his eyes were rolled back into his head. He'd die on this rooftop if somebody didn't get fluids into him quickly. I grabbed the skinny teen beneath his armpits, lifted him onto my shoulders, and carried him down six flights of stairs. Whenever I tried to catch my breath, I could smell the putrid stench of alcohol and vomit expelled from the young man's body.

"You got vomit all over you," my astute partner remarked as I laid the teen on the sidewalk.

When the paramedics arrived, they ran an IV into his arm before strapping on an oxygen mask to his colorless face.

"How much would you say he had to drink?" the EMT asked.

"A lot more than he could handle," I replied, watching them load the stretcher into the ambulance.

When I returned to the radio car, Shit Can Sammy admonished me for doing my job.

"I can't believe you got us involved with this nonsense." He pointed at the clock on the dashboard.

Unfortunately for Shit Can Sammy, the night was far from over. The teenager was our responsibility until a relative was located. Besides, I wasn't about to let a child on death's door go to the emergency room alone.

"Fuck you, Sammy. We're taking a ride to the hospital," I replied.

Lights and sirens, I followed the ambulance to Montefiore Hospital over the objections of my useless partner. When we arrived, the EMTs rushed the unconscious teen into the back of the emergency room.

"How long would you say he was left out in the cold?" the ER nurse asked, shining a penlight into his eyes.

"I don't know, probably a while," I replied.

"His pulse is weak," she shouted, trying to get a doctor's attention.

"Do you think he's going to make it?" I asked the battle-hardened ER nurse.

"It looks like his kidneys have shut down. It's in God's hands."

A few minutes later, the boy's panicked mother raced into the emergency room, searching for her son.

"I knew something was wrong when he didn't come home by eleven p.m.," the hysterical middle-aged woman said.

While I tried to calm her down, I saw my heartless partner staring at his watch. On the ride back to the precinct, I had to listen to Shit Can Sammy gripe about working past his bedtime.

"I told you I couldn't work late," he complained.

"Listen, Sammy, don't take this the wrong way, but I'd rather spend the night sitting with a DOA than work with you again," I replied.

That would be the last time Shit Can Sammy and I worked together. When I asked our roll call police administrative aide not to pair us again, she laughed. "Don't worry, the feeling is mutual."

A few weeks later, I spotted the unconscious teen hanging out with several of his buddies in front of his building. He looked much better than the last time I saw him. That day, he was full of piss and vinegar, clowning around with his friends. I pulled up to the front of the building and called him over to the radio car.

"Hey, you. Come here," I said, pointing to the skinny teen.

He muttered something, causing his buddies to laugh as he approached the radio car. Joe Cool was putting on a show for his friends.

"What?" He leaned into the radio car.

"Remember me?" I asked.

"No," he snapped, looking over his shoulder at his snickering friends.

"I'm the guy who saved your life a few weeks ago." I gestured to the top of the building.

"Oh, shit." He lowered his head into the car to get a better look at me.

"Are those the guys that left you up there to die?" I asked.

The young man looked at the ground as I lectured him about his choice of friends.

"After you passed out, they went home and never gave you a second thought. The only reason I was up there was because one of your neighbors called the police about all the noise you were making up there," I said.

The kid looked like he wanted to cry when I reminded him about what he had put his mother through. I gave him a lot to think about while his friends continued to clown around in the background.

"Thank you for saving my life." He reached into the radio car to shake my hand.

"Listen, I'm not your father, but I'm going to give you some advice, and I hope you take it."

"Sure," the young man replied.

"You need to find some new friends," I said, pointing to his posse.

"Thank you again," the boy said before returning to the group.

As we drove away, my partner turned to me and asked, "Do you think that sank in?"

"It's in God's hands," I replied.

That would be the last time I saw the troubled teen.

Hopefully, he turned his life around and grew up to be a productive member of society. From what I could gather, his mother loved him dearly, crying and pacing the emergency room floor. He came dangerously close to death that night. I hope that was enough to scare him straight.

COORS LIGHT QUARTET

As teenagers, my friends and I would hang around the neighborhood deli, searching for a morally flexible adult to purchase beer for us. It didn't take long for someone to pity our crew, and before you knew it, we were in the schoolyard sipping brewskis. Eventually, the cops would come along and pour out our beer before sending us on our way. I couldn't understand why they were busting our balls. After all, we weren't bothering anyone.

"Don't they have better things to do?" I'd ask, watching my beer go down the drain. *When I become a cop, I'll never bother teenagers having a good time,* I'd tell myself, promising not to become a hypocrite after I took the oath to protect and serve. By the ripe age of sixteen, I had life all figured out.

Ten years later, on a brisk October evening, my partner and I were riding around in an unmarked police car in the Riverdale section of the Bronx. I loved working in the plainclothes detail. Our dented Ford LTD with dark-tinted windows looked like a beat-up gypsy cab. The nondescript car was far from stealthy, but it gave us a few valuable seconds to observe a crime unfold before the bad guys spotted us.

We were hanging around a shopping plaza after a gang of rooftop burglars had hit several commercial establishments in the precinct.

My partner and I reasoned the Riverdale shopping center, which housed a bank and a supermarket, would make an excellent target for a burglary.

I drove to the back of the supermarket and spotted several teenagers hanging around the loading dock. When we drove up, the boys grabbed several shopping bags from the ground, getting ready to flee.

"Guys, don't make us chase you," my partner shouted over the PA system, causing them to stop.

"What are you guys doing?" I asked.

"Drinking," one boy replied.

"How much beer do you have?"

"Two six packs," said the boy in a red and blue New York Giants jacket.

Although underage, the four teens didn't appear to be drunk.

"Are you going to take our beer?" one asked.

"Do you want me to?" I replied, causing them to laugh.

The boys relaxed and asked my partner and me about the police department.

"How long have you guys been cops? Have you ever shot someone?" and countless other silly questions that brought back fond memories.

A few years earlier, I was doing the same thing, picking the cops' brains as they poured out my beer.

"Are you guys thinking about becoming cops?" I asked.

"Yeah," the quartet answered in unison.

"Don't you guys don't have school tomorrow?" I asked.

"No, sir. We're off for Columbus Day," one boy replied.

"Listen to me. When you're done with those Coors Lights, I want you to clean up your mess," I instructed.

"No problem, Officer," the group replied.

"Boys, stay out of trouble," I cautioned.

The teens thanked us for not pouring out their beer before my partner and I drove off in search of our gang of burglars.

"Nice kids," my partner noted.

"They remind me of myself ten years ago," I replied.

The next weekend, we received a robbery call at West 263rd Street and Riverdale Avenue. Four white males had robbed a bus driver at gunpoint. The perps took fifty dollars off the victim before fleeing south on Riverdale Avenue. One suspect wore a New York Giants jacket.

"Look at those guys over there," my partner said, pointing at four boys walking down Riverdale Avenue.

"That's a New York Giants jacket," I said, rolling up on the group.

"Police, don't move!" I shouted, jumping from our unmarked car and stopping the gang at gunpoint. Stunned, the group of teens complied as we ushered them against the wall of a building.

"Don't fucking move," I said as we patted them down for weapons.

"Officer, you don't remember us?" one boy asked.

"Remember you? From where?" I said.

"The other night. You stopped us in the back of the Food Emporium for drinking beer," he replied.

"Where are you guys coming from?" I asked.

Nobody wanted to answer that question.

Within seconds, my partner recovered a black Daisy BB gun from the boy wearing the New York Giants football jacket.

"Guys, you're in a lot of trouble," I said as my partner requested the robbery victim be brought over to view the suspects.

Minutes later, a radio car arrived with the shaken bus driver. He exited the police car and approached the four boys standing against the building.

"That's them!" he shouted as my partner and I handcuffed the teens.

We squeezed the four boys into the back seat of our unmarked car for the ride to the precinct.

"Officer, can you give us a break?" one boy begged.

"Guys, you just robbed a bus driver at gunpoint. How am I supposed to give you a break?" I asked.

"Officer, it's a BB gun," the kid in the New York Giants jacket pointed out.

"How is the victim supposed to know that? Guys, you stole someone's money under the threat of violence," I replied.

Besides the recovered BB gun, a fifty-dollar bill was found inside one of the teen's pockets. It was an airtight case against the four Catholic high school boys who graduated from drinking beer in the back of the Food Emporium to armed robbery.

The middle-aged bus driver looked like he was going to have a heart attack. After popping several nitroglycerin pills, he calmed down to explain how the robbery went down.

As he waited for his shift to begin, he noticed the four teens hanging around the bus stop. They pounded on the bus doors, demanding he let them inside. After explaining he wouldn't be leaving for another fifteen minutes, the boy in the New York Giants jacket pulled out a black pistol and shoved it through the folding doors, demanding money. Terrified, the bus driver compiled, slipping a fifty-dollar bill through the door while another teen snatched it before fleeing down Riverdale Avenue.

"Those boys are very lucky to be alive," the bus driver explained.

"What do you mean?" I asked.

"That's not my route. I was filling in for Bill. He called in sick this evening."

"Who's Bill?"

"Bill's a retired correction officer. He doesn't fool around," the victim replied.

"I'm guessing Bill carries a gun?" I said.

"Sometimes two," the bus driver replied, shaking his head.

When I explained to the boys they were lucky to be alive, they shouted at the ringleader in the New York Giants jacket for jeopardizing their futures.

While being fingerprinted, one teen asked, "Officer, will this arrest prevent me from becoming a police officer?"

"What do you think?" I replied.

When we arrived at Bronx Central Booking, reality set in.

"I thought we were going to Spofford (juvenile detention center)?" one asked.

"You're sixteen years old."

"What does that mean?" the boy replied.

"That means you're in the major leagues. You boys are charged as adults," I said while opening the steel door to the building.

I felt bad for the felonious four as we entered the concrete dungeon. Inside, the quartet followed my partner and me around like lost puppies. After removing their handcuffs, we walked them down a narrow hallway leading to the bullpen or holding cells.

Warming up in the bullpen was an all-star cast of drunks and dirtbags arrested throughout the Bronx. The teenage boys would share the large, filthy cell with their new roommates for the weekend.

"Take off your belts and shoelaces," the grizzled correction officer shouted before tossing them manilla envelopes.

"Why do you want our shoelaces?" one boy asked.

"We don't want you hanging yourself," he replied, stuffing their belongings into the envelope.

When the envelopes were full, the correction officer motioned the four boys into the large cell before locking them in.

"Good luck, fellas," I said outside the jail cell.

"Do you mean that?" one boy asked, his fingers gripping the grimy steel bars.

"Listen, guys, before tonight, I liked you. But now we're on opposite sides of the line," I said before walking away.

The four childhood friends spent the weekend in jail before being released to their parents on Monday morning.

Like every arrest I made, I tried not to think too much about what happened behind the scenes. That was up to lawyers to figure out. I could offer my advice, but in the end, it was up to the criminal justice system to mete out justice.

A few days later, my partner and I received a subpoena to testify before a Bronx grand jury for the robbery arrests.

"You will not believe this. The four defendants want to testify," the district attorney said.

"That's unusual," I replied.

"It sure is. If they decide to go to trial, I can cross-examine their grand jury testimony," the district attorney laughed.

"Do they have representation?"

"Each of them has an attorney."

"Then why are they letting them testify?"

"I believe their defense will be that it was a prank gone wrong."

"I'm sure it was. But that doesn't change the fact that they scared the shit out of a bus driver and stole his money."

"I've seen this legal strategy tried before. It rarely works," the district attorney explained.

"Well, whatever story they want to tell, the grand jury won't buy it," I said.

After my partner and I finished testifying, we ran into the boys flanked by their parents and attorneys waiting by the elevators.

The rowdy teens had cleaned up since the last time I saw them. Today, they looked like altar boys in their Catholic high school uniforms. The four miscreants gave me a nod before looking at the floor in embarrassment. It was obvious they were having a bad week. Spending a weekend in Bronx Central booking would put Kelly Ripa in a bad mood.

"How are you guys doing?" I asked.

"They're in a lot of trouble," one parent grumbled.

"I know. They've made a terrible mistake," I replied.

"Mistake? They've ruined their lives!" he shouted.

Unfazed by the awkward conversation, the defense attorneys led the group into an elevator.

"I guess the meter is running," my partner joked while we waited for the next elevator.

Telling the grand jury their side of the story didn't help their case.

The four boys were indicted for robbery and criminal possession of a weapon. Six months later, everyone took a plea deal to a felony conviction and several years of probation. During my NYPD career, I was involved in thousands of arrests. I never gave many of them a second thought.

Thirty years later, those arrests haunt me.

Four young boys with promising futures became convicted felons. Should I have confiscated their beer and brought them into the precinct a few nights earlier? A late-night phone call to their parents might have resulted in punishment that kept them off the street that fateful evening.

Ultimately, those boys made a terrible decision with long-lasting consequences. Hopefully, they learned from their mistakes and turned their lives around. Looking back, having my beer poured out was the best thing to happen to me. I didn't realize getting rousted by the cops was a preventative measure that kept me from getting too comfortable with my newfound testosterone. Years later, while working in the Narcotics Division, I ran into a former foe who was now a lieutenant. He and his partner often hassled my friends and me when we got out of hand in the back of the local schoolyard.

"Lieutenant, do you remember me?" I asked.

Barely picking up his head, the salty Narcotics supervisor replied, "Should I?"

"When I was a teenager, you and your partner would bust my balls for drinking beer," I said.

The lieutenant took off his readers and studied my face. "Well, I see you turned out okay," he said before returning to his newspaper.

Like the four teenagers I arrested, I, too, had been a rebellious teen looking to make my mark on the world. Fortunately, the cops saved me from crossing the point of no return.

Like my father would tell me, one bad decision can ruin your life.

CHAPTER 6

MEDALS, MORONS & CRYOTHERAPY

The next time you see a uniformed member of the New York City Police Department, check out the leather rack adorned with colorful bars above their shield. The medal rack or "rack" is where NYPD members display their list of accomplishments. As a rookie police officer, I'd marvel at the veteran cop's different colored medals. I didn't know what they were for, but I wanted them. Cops are like kids in the schoolyard, always sizing each other up. Rookie patrolmen mimic veteran cops the way a ten-year-old tries to shave with his father's razor.

NYPD medals have different meanings, and some carry more weight than others. The three that stand out are the Medal of Honor, Valor, and the Police Combat Cross. When you see a lime green or navy-blue bar above someone's shield, you know they were in a gunfight, and the other party isn't around anymore. I've seen NYPD members with those medals pinned to their chests walk through a crowd of cops like Moses parting the Red Sea. When those guys walk into a precinct, the place goes silent. It's like an old Western when a gunfighter enters a saloon.

Ceremonies when you receive a medal are rare. Ninety-nine percent of the time, you buy your own after filling out a lengthy form. You could solve the DB Cooper hijacking case, but if you don't fill out the proper paperwork, you're not getting a medal. And filling out the ridiculous form doesn't guarantee you anything.

When I was a young cop running around the Bronx making felony arrests, I didn't know how the process worked.

While processing a robbery arrest one afternoon, my lieutenant offered some advice. "You should write this up for a commendation," he said.

"Lieutenant, how do I go about doing that?"

"Fill this out and submit it to the committee," he replied, handing me a form.

"Committee?" I asked.

"The precinct medal committee."

I had worked in the precinct for over a year and had never heard of a medal committee. Who were these people? Where did they meet? And what criteria were required to serve on this mysterious committee? A few days later, I typed out the form and delivered it to my lieutenant.

"Okay, great," he said, before tossing it in an open drawer on his desk.

I walked out of his office, confused as ever. I didn't want to be a pain in the ass, so I kept my mouth shut. A few weeks later, an envelope from the medal committee appeared in my mailbox. Inside was a folded copy of the form I submitted with the word *denied* stamped across the top in red ink.

Denied? What the fuck?

By all accounts, it was an excellent arrest. An armed robbery suspect was captured without a shot fired. The arrest helped the Bronx Robbery Squad close out multiple cases. Something wasn't right here. With a little digging, I unearthed the identities of the precinct medal committee.

"Are you kidding me?" I asked, waving the form in the precinct auxiliary coordinator's chubby face.

"Well, we can't give out a commendation for every arrest submitted," the pear-shaped cop replied.

"Maybe you should get off your ass once in a while and see how the other half lives," I shouted.

Now everything made sense. This so-called committee was a bunch of fat, lazy cops who never left the station house.

Our commanding officer had stocked this think tank with a cord of dead wood. It was a who's who of kiss asses and empty suits that hadn't made an arrest in years. As juvenile as it sounds, something as trivial as a medal is a morale boost for the department's rank-and-file members.

Rarely will the average street cop get an "atta boy" for a job well done. A few days after unloading on the auxiliary coordinator, my lieutenant called me into his office.

"I hear you're not happy with how the process works," he laughed, holding a copy of my denied request.

"Lieutenant, you thought the arrest was worthy of departmental recognition."

"I did," he replied, examining the document.

"I'm confused."

"Vic, let me give you a little advice. Next time, be a little more creative with your writing and learn how to play the game."

"What game?"

"If you ever want to get anywhere on this job, you're going to have to kiss ass occasionally," he explained.

I was a cop, not William Shakespeare, and I wasn't kissing anyone's ass. I had no use for brown-nosing cops who sat around the precinct laughing at the commanding officers' bad jokes.

"So I guess that's it," I replied.

"No, I'm overruling their decision."

"Lou?" I asked.

"You'll get your medal," he replied.

My lieutenant respected hard-working cops. He often intervened when he thought they weren't getting a fair shake. The next thing he said would stay with me for the rest of my NYPD career.

"Vic, I can't do this every time you have an issue with the medal committee."

"Why not?"

"Because that would rub them the wrong way," the lieutenant explained.

"Who cares if it rubs them the wrong way?"

"The commanding officer does," the lieutenant replied.

That put everything into perspective. It wasn't about me or my stupid medal. It was precinct politics and not upsetting the applecart. Overruling the committee's decision would leave a bad taste in their mouths.

No fiefdom wants to lose what little power it has over its serfs. I battled the useless committee for years when I applied for a medal. I didn't care. I made so many arrests they had to approve some of them for fear they weren't doing their jobs. I just outworked them. Why would anyone go through all that trouble for a silly medal? It all boils down to ego. Times have changed, but human behavior remains the same.

After winning a gun battle, gunfighters added a notch to their belts. TGI Friday employees receive a decorative pin when they get an order right. Everyone (including me) wants to be recognized for their accomplishments. A medal rack tells an NYPD member's story. That brings us back to the prestigious Medal of Honor, Valor, and the Police Combat Cross.

Every cop is aware of their mortality. Those particular medals show you can handle yourself when the shit hits the fan. In a world where the next shift could be your last, those are the people you can count on. For whatever reason, there was never a shortage of immortal cops in the borough of Brooklyn.

When I'd go to Brooklyn to work the West Indian Day parade or the Coney Island detail, there would always be more than a few prestigious medals floating around. You could hear a pin drop when those cops entered a room. Everyone in the department knows what those horizontal bars mean and affords those NYPD members the utmost respect.

After a while, the public noticed who was doing their job and who wasn't. So, the department began handing out faux medals to even the playing field. The Pistol Expert Medal or Community Service Commendation might look nice, but they didn't carry any weight inside the station house.

My favorite is the Unit Citation Medal. It's awarded to a precinct or specialized unit for its outstanding accomplishments. What those accomplishments are is hard to say, but everyone in the command gets one. It's the equivalent of a grammar school class participation award. Community affairs officer, roll call flunky, and precinct broom, step up and get your medal.

Another reason NYPD members write up their heroics is for the points they receive on promotional exams. Each medal has a value of something like 0.116th of a point. It might not sound like much, but if you can string enough medals together to earn an eighth of a point, you just moved yourself up on the sergeant's list. You have to pass the exam to use your points, but those medals can make a tremendous difference when you get promoted.

Unfortunately, some NYPD members have lied or embellished to get a medal. Defense attorneys will subpoena medal requests and compare them to arrest reports and grand jury testimony. If they don't line up, you lose your job.

It's rare, but some cops choose not to write up their arrests. They either don't have the time or ego for the silly process. After I got promoted to detective, I was finished. I was in plainclothes ninety-five percent of the time, so what was the point? The next time you see a uniformed NYPD member, check out their medal rack. You might look at them differently now.

START YOUR ENGINES

In the early nineties, automatic car starters were the rage in New York City. Everyone wanted the luxury of warming up their vehicle from inside their home. With the push of a button, you could start your car from a block away. One snowy afternoon, I noticed a detective staring out the window of our office.

"What are you doing, Raul? I asked.

"Hey, Vic, watch the look on the woman's face when I start my car," he laughed.

"Raul, don't be an asshole," I replied as he pointed the remote out the window toward his car.

As the elderly woman walked between two parked cars, one lurched forward, pinning her between the two vehicles.

"Holy shit, I must have left my car in gear!" Raul shouted.

"Your car is a standard shift?" I laughed.

"Yeah. I gotta get down there," Raul said, throwing on his jacket and racing out the door.

"The automatic starter is worth more than your car," I laughed.

Leaving your car in gear can be quite expensive. The startled woman suffered a broken hip and sued the detective for damages due to his perpetual PT Cruiser.

CHEAP ASSES

One former supervisor was one of the cheapest people I've ever known. Every morning before we went out on patrol, he'd ask, "Vic, are ya hungry?" Then, he would direct me to a roach coach parked in a factory parking lot. After ordering a coffee and a buttered roll, the grandiose sergeant would snatch the check from my hand and say, "I got this, Vic. You get lunch later." He'd hand the cashier a five-dollar bill for both orders.

Later that day, I'd pay for his Italian combo and a large Diet Coke that exceeded my two-dollar breakfast. I didn't care. He was a great supervisor and instrumental in my career. I never minded paying a few extra bucks when the cheap ass was a friend. With every friendship, there is a give and take, and a few dollars here and there wouldn't hurt anybody. When the cheap ass is an asshole, then you mind.

Everybody knows an asshole. That loveable pain in the ass who loves to state the obvious. The cheap uncle that gives out two-dollar bills for birthday presents or the dreaded Susan B.

Anthony dollar as a Christmas gift. Before you call me a misogynist, try pulling that handsome woman out of your pocket to pay for a big gulp at the local 7-11. Every asshole has a cheap parlor trick they love to pull out at social functions. One such asshole was a lieutenant I worked for. Occasionally, he would meet the platoon for drinks at the local pub after work. Clutching his beer, he'd monitor the bar like a card counter at the blackjack table, waiting to make his move.

"Oh, I got this," he'd say when it was his turn to buy a round of drinks. He'd dig through his pockets before prying open an empty wallet.

"Jesus, guys, I don't have any cash on me," he'd say, finishing his beer and leaving the pub.

Another move he had was using a hundred-dollar bill to pay for items that cost under five dollars. Most of the time, business owners around the precinct let the uniformed lieutenant have the item for free instead of breaking the large bill. This schmuck would pull a hundred-dollar bill out of his pocket at a Dollar Tree.

AN UNCOMFORTABLE RIDE

Throughout my NYPD career, I couldn't believe some of the bizarre stories I'd hear floating around the station house. "There is no way that could have happened," I'd laugh after hearing about some NYPD member doing something ridiculous that landed them in hot water. Sometimes, it's an error in judgment. Other times, it boils down to sheer laziness.

My friend's mother told me one such story after she was pickpocketed at her local bank. Believe it or not, pickpocketing is an art. It takes years of practice before mastering the skill to slide a hand into a handbag or back pocket undetected. After withdrawing two hundred dollars from the teller's window, the woman was jostled by two well-dressed men who quickly fled the bank.

Luckily, another customer observed the two pickpockets removing cash from her bag. After alerting the police, the two con men were captured a few blocks away by a patrolman who wanted nothing to do with the arrest. From the onset, the snarky cop tried to talk my friend's mother out of pressing charges.

"Are you sure these are the men that stole your money?" he asked after she identified the pair.

"Yes, I'm sure. Didn't they have my two hundred dollars in a cash envelope?" the woman asked.

"Well, these cases often get dismissed," the cop replied.

It seemed odd to the shaken victim that a police officer would try to discourage her from pressing charges. After all, wasn't it his job to arrest criminals?

After she put her foot down, the cop agreed to pick her up in a few hours and drive her to the courthouse to file charges.

The woman sat by her phone all afternoon, awaiting further instructions. Several hours later, a police car tapped its siren in front of her house.

That's odd. I thought he would call first, she thought, grabbing her jacket and keys.

When the middle-aged housewife stepped outside, she saw her two muggers seated in the backseat of the patrol car.

"Why the hell would you bring them to my house?" she shouted at the arresting officer.

"Oh, don't worry about them. They're handcuffed," the cop replied, looking over his shoulder.

"Now they know where I live," she said.

The lazy cop turned to his prisoners and said, "Guys, I don't want you coming back here." He then reached across the front seat to unlock the passenger door.

The half-assed warning didn't put my friend's mother at ease. "They're criminals. They won't listen to you," she shouted.

Afraid of repercussions, she turned around and began walking back to her house.

"You might as well take off their handcuffs because I'm not pressing charges," she said.

Leaving the two handcuffed prisoners unattended, the cop jumped out of the radio car and followed the woman to her doorstep.

"I got stuck with this collar, and now you don't want to press charges?" he shouted.

"Drop dead," she replied before slamming the door in the cop's face.

When she told me the story, I couldn't believe it.

"Are you kidding me?" I asked.

"Victor, I couldn't believe how unprofessional that police officer was," she said.

I had known the woman since childhood and didn't think she would make up a story. I knew some lazy cops that would squash the occasional arrest. But bringing two perps to a victim's house was beyond anything I could fathom. The story was so unbelievable I asked a friend who worked in the precinct if that was possible.

"Oh, it's more than possible," he laughed after I dropped the cop's name.

"What's this guy's story?" I asked.

"Which story would you like to hear?" my friend replied.

For twenty minutes, I heard a litany of unbelievable tales about a lazy cop who didn't see a problem arranging a carpool of criminals at his victim's house.

"You would think a guy that's been kicked out of two precincts already would get the hint and fly straight," my friend said.

I told my buddy that the woman was thinking about making a civilian complaint against the cop, which prompted him to say: "Oh, I think she should."

The NYPD takes civilian complaints (CCRB's)seriously. CCRBs are supposed to keep track of cops with anger management issues. Most active cops accumulate civilian complaints for doing their jobs. Civilian complaints are often levied from those looking to even the score with their arresting officer. When a cop acquires too many civilian complaints, it can prevent them from working in a specialized unit. Once the department considers you toxic, there is little chance for advancement.

For another NYPD member to recommend filing a civilian complaint meant this cop had to be a total piece of shit.

"You think so?" I asked.

"Vic, drive her to the precinct, and I'll take the report. She'd be doing every cop in the station house a favor."

I wasn't doing that. I had stuck my nose in the mess far enough and explained to the woman that she had to go to the precinct and file a report if she wanted to pursue the matter.

Understandably, she had little confidence in the NYPD after being victimized twice and declined to pursue the matter.

About a year later, I heard the lazy cop had once again gotten himself into trouble. This time he was involved with an insurance fraud ring that filed phony vehicle accident reports. After his arrest and suspension, it was just a matter of time before the department terminated him.

When I told my friend's mother the story, she said, "I'd love to give him a ride to court!"

QUICK CHANGE

The older I get, the more I find myself explaining things to young people. I never signed on as an educator, but sometimes I have no choice. This makes it challenging when dealing with millennials. Millennials think the world began in the 1990s, so you have to find a reference to which they can relate.

I'm a huge proponent of cryotherapy. I go to a sauna several times a week for cold treatments. I know this may sound radical for some, but stepping into a cryosauna at minus 165 degrees below zero for three and a half minutes has done wonders for me. The treatments keep aches, pains, and inflammation to a minimum. Before stepping into the chamber, I go to a dressing room and change into a pair of shorts, gloves, a skullcap, and a pair of Crocs.

One day after a session, the early twenties manager told me, "I'm always amazed at how fast you're able to change in and out of your clothes."

"I just had a flashback to my NYPD career," I replied.

As a rookie cop, I'd marvel at the old-timers breezing through the station house minutes before roll call. There was no urgency as they made their rounds, chit-chatting with the other cops before disappearing into the locker room. Seconds later, they were popping out of a stairwell dressed in their police uniforms. "How the hell did he do that?" I'd ask like a child watching a magic trick. After a couple of years, I, too, was changing in and out of my uniform in a matter of seconds.

After telling the story to the curious cryo manager, she asked, "Why didn't you wear your uniform to work?"

I had to explain to the young lady that showing up at the station house dressed in your police uniform could give your coworkers the impression you were wearing a wire.

"Have you seen *Serpico*?" I asked.

"Does he have a membership here?" she replied.

CHAPTER 7

CREATIVE CAR THIEVES

Unfortunately, most victims of auto theft never get to meet the scumbag who stole their car. Unlike a robbery, where you're confronted by an assailant demanding money, auto theft is impersonal. One morning, you leave the house to retrieve your vehicle and find an empty parking space. You call the police. They'll take a report and offer little hope of finding your pride and joy. Now it's time to call your insurance company. While on hold, you try to picture the son of a bitch who stole your ride. More than likely, it was a young punk in a hooded sweatshirt jimmying your door lock before vanishing with your vehicle.

While that is the most plausible scenario, there are other ways to steal your car.

Instead of driving around all night, lugging a bag of tools, these thieves are creative. Forged documents, bad checks, and unattended car keys are just a few ways con artists can steal your car. Paper criminals are more difficult to combat because catching them in the act is next to impossible. They reply to online advertisements or appear at car dealerships looking to kick the tires of an expensive ride. Well-dressed and polite, they say all the right things while providing a bad check or stolen identity before riding off into the sunset with your vehicle. It takes a day or two until the bad news hits. Then you feel like a fool. How could you have been so stupid? You handed some scumbag the keys to your car.

Identifying the mastermind of a confidence game is like searching for fool's gold. Fake names and bogus addresses can lead down countless rabbit holes designed to bog you down until you give up. You're often chasing a ghost or Keyser Söze-like character who never uses the same identity twice. For the detective handling the case, that's when the fun begins.

THREE SIDES TO EVERY STORY

"So, what do you want to talk about?" I asked.

"Detective, I know what you're thinking," the young man said, peeking through the steel bars of the Nineteenth Precinct's holding cell.

"Listen, if you could read minds, I wouldn't be standing here with you," I replied.

I wasn't in the mood for games. Working weekends at the Auto Crime Division meant bouncing around the city, debriefing prisoners. Sometimes, the jailhouse meet and greets led to valuable information. But mostly, it was a bouillabaisse of bullshit served by two-bit street hustlers trying to avoid jail time. I planned to spend the morning catching up on paperwork, not trekking into Manhattan to interview a car thief.

"You told your arresting officer you wanted to talk. So talk,"

"I know I'm just another black man in a jail cell to you. But I swear to God I didn't steal that car."

I got lied to all the time. That was part of the job. By this point in my career, I had heard it all. But this had a different vibe. The mid-twenties prisoner was an open nerve, pacing the jail cell like a caged tiger. Before we got started, I had to get him to focus on the topic at hand.

"Look, I'm willing to hear what you have to say, but leave the race card in your pocket," I replied.

"That car is mine. I paid for it."

"Fair enough. If you want to talk to me about what happened today, I must read you your rights," I explained.

Before I could read the last line on the Miranda card, the anxious man started spilling his guts. "I bought a Lexus from a used car lot near my girlfriend's house in Brooklyn," he said.

"Did they give you a title?" I asked.

"Yeah, a New Jersey title."

"Do you have it?"

"No, I turned it into the DMV when I registered the vehicle."

"You registered the Lexus?" I asked.

It's rare to register a stolen vehicle. It's happened before, but usually, the DMV clerk catches it when they run the vehicle identification number before issuing a set of license plates.

"Detective, I walked on that car lot and paid twenty thousand dollars cash for that vehicle," the prisoner said.

"Give me a few minutes," I replied.

I hunted down the arresting officer in the precinct lunchroom, wolfing down a slice of pizza.

"So, what's the deal with this arrest?" I asked.

"I saw a Lexus RX 330 double parked on Lexington Avenue. I started writing a double-parking ticket, and the perp came running out of a store to move it. When I told him it was too late, he got mouthy, so I ran the VIN (vehicle identification number), and it came back reported stolen from Ridgefield Park, New Jersey," the cop explained.

"Did he say anything?" I asked.

"He hasn't stopped talking. He insists he bought the vehicle from a used car lot in Brooklyn," the arresting officer replied.

I returned to the holding cell and explained the next step in the process to the prisoner.

"I'll look into it. But if I drive out to this car lot in Brooklyn and find out you're bullshitting me, I will tell the district attorney to throw the book at you."

"So I have to spend the night in jail?" he asked.

"I can't wave a magic wand and dismiss your case because you're telling me you're innocent. I told you I would look into it," I explained.

I took down the man's information and told him I'd be in touch, provided he told the truth about the stolen vehicle. Otherwise, I'd be phoning the district attorney tasked with prosecuting this case.

"We'll talk again," he replied.

As a rule of thumb, there are three sides to every story. What he said, what she said, and what really happened. At this point, I had one side coming from inside a jail cell. This mystery would take a little investigating to get to the truth.

"Do you believe this guy's story?" my skeptical partner asked on the drive back to our office.

"I'm not sure, but he seemed ticked off."

"What do you think happened?"

"I don't know. But somehow, he got his hands on a Jersey title and used it to register a stolen vehicle."

"It's probably a phony title," my partner reasoned.

"Maybe, but why register a stolen car in your own name?"

"This sounds like a clusterfuck. You think this is worth the trouble of going out to Brooklyn?" he asked.

My partner had a point. We both had heavy caseloads and were expected to make several arrests a month. If there was a dip in activity, our lieutenant wouldn't want to hear that we killed a day on a wild goose chase through Brooklyn.

Investigating this car caper would be time-consuming. There is constant pressure in law enforcement to produce results. Some detectives avoid complicated investigations and pick the low-lying fruit to get an easy arrest. Schlepping out to Brooklyn to hear another side of this story was far from a sure thing.

There are no shortcuts to Brooklyn. You can speed, levitate, or have a police escort, and it will still take you over an hour to get there.

Bright and early the following morning, my partner and I set sail for the borough of churches. Coming from the Bronx, I crossed two bridges and battled the Belt Parkway before arriving at a shitty used car lot in the Canarsie section of the borough.

"Mohammed Motors?" my partner laughed, pointing to the rusting sign hanging off the side of the fence.

The gravel lot was filled with banged-up, high-mileage vehicles with cheesy slogans on their windshields. The sounds of ripped plastic flags flapped in the frigid January air as my partner and I made our way to an old trailer in the back of the lot.

"Can I help you?" asked the man with hairy knuckles sitting behind a desk.

"I'd like to speak to the owner," I asked.

"That's me," the man replied.

I took out my detective shield for him to examine and said, "I'm Detective Ferrari from the Auto Crime Division."

"I run a clean lot," the man protested.

"I can see that," I replied, watching a large cockroach climb the wall behind his head.

"What can I help you with?" he asked.

"I need to see your MV-50 book," I replied.

An MV-50 is a form that accompanies the sale of a used vehicle. Car dealers are required to record every transaction in their MV-50 book. The books are subject to inspection to ensure the business complies with the rules and regulations of a second-hand car dealer.

"You won't find any funny business here," he said, digging through a file cabinet.

"Relax, Mohammed. I'm sure this is a big misunderstanding," I replied.

While inspecting the thick MV-50 book, Mohammed began probing me for information. "If you tell me what you're looking for, maybe I can save you some time."

"Have you purchased or sold a Lexus RX 330 in the past two months?" I asked.

"Nope," he snapped back.

"You seem sure of that," I said.

"Detective, I'm here seven days a week. If something comes on this lot, I know about it," Mohammed replied.

"Did you sell a car to this man?" I asked, handing him a photocopy of the defendant's driver's license and the vehicle identification number of the stolen Lexus. Mohammed studied the documents as if his life depended on it.

"Detective, I've never seen that man before in my life, and that car has never been on my lot," he replied.

If I were playing poker, I would have folded. According to Mohammed, his books, like his conscience, were clean. Unable to find the stolen Lexus in his MV-50 books, I thanked him for his time before exiting the dilapidated trailer.

"Next time, call. I could have saved you the trouble of driving down here," the hospitable used car dealer mocked as I snaked through the lot.

"What do you think?" my partner asked.

"I think Mohammed is a shifty character."

"You think he's hiding something?"

"I do. But I don't know what it is."

"Out of all the two-bit used car lots in Brooklyn, why would that kid send us here?" my partner asked.

Debating my next move, I spotted a black Lexus RX 330 in the back of the used car lot.

"Is that what I think it is?" I asked.

"Sure is," my partner replied as we walked to the back of the lot.

While writing down the Lexus vehicle identification number, my partner shouted, "There's another one over there!"

"For a guy who seemed sure of his inventory, these two must have slipped his mind," I laughed while running the vehicle identification numbers over my portable radio.

Like the Lexus RX 330 that landed a man in a Manhattan jail cell, the two luxury SUVs on Mohammed's used car lot were also reported stolen.

"This motherfucker," I laughed, walking back to the trailer.

Seconds later, my partner and I were interrupting Mohammed's lunch.

"What's the problem now?" he asked, fiddling with his falafel.

"Mohammed, you got problems," I replied.

"What are you talking about?" he asked, licking the grease from his fingers.

"For starters, you have two stolen Lexus SUVs sitting on your lot."

"I didn't know they were stolen," Mohammed replied.

"I asked you five minutes ago if you had purchased or sold a Lexus RX 330 in the last two months."

"They just came in today," Mohammed nervously replied.

"Why aren't they in your books?"

For a guy who couldn't stop talking, Mohammed became silent.

"Mohammed?" I asked.

"I bought them from a couple of Nigerian guys," he confessed.

"How many vehicles have you purchased from them?

"Six," Mohammed replied.

"Where's the paperwork?" I asked.

Mohammed reached into a desk drawer and handed me two vehicle titles.

As I examined the documents, Mohammed rambled on. "They started coming around last month selling Lexus SUVs," he explained.

"They always had a title for the vehicle?"

"Always. How can these vehicles be stolen if they had titles?" Mohammed asked.

That was a good question. Unfortunately for Mohammed, I had a few of my own. Like why didn't he keep a record of the purchase and sale of the Lexus SUVs?

Every vehicle on Mohammed's lot was in his MV-50 book except for the six he purchased from the Nigerians. Mohammed had to suspect something wasn't right with these vehicles.

"Mohammed, I'm going to give you one chance to come clean about this," I said.

Mohammed explained the two men came to his lot once a week with a Lexus SUV to sell. After negotiating a price (twenty-five percent below market value), the men produced a title and set of keys for the vehicle.

"And this didn't raise your suspicions?" I asked.

"No, why?"

"Do you have a way of getting in touch with these guys?

"No, they just show up when they have a vehicle to sell," Mohammed replied.

"So let me ask you again. Did you sell this guy a Lexus?" I asked, handing him a photocopy of the young man's driver's license.

Mohammed studied the photo once again before nodding his head. "Yeah," he replied.

I heard enough. The guy in the holding cell of the Nineteenth Precinct was telling the truth. I left Mohammed Motors with two Lexus trucks and their owner in handcuffs. Mohammed would come in handy to testify against his Nigerian business associates, provided I could find them. The following morning, I called the victims of the stolen Lexus SUVs to hear their side of the story.

All had similar experiences after placing their vehicle for sale on Craigslist. Within twenty-four hours, they were contacted by a man with a heavy accent. The following day, the potential buyer and his mechanic came over to inspect their vehicle. Both men were well-dressed and polite. They asked the usual questions you'd expect to hear from someone interested in purchasing a used vehicle. After kicking the tires and examining the maintenance records, the African businessman agreed to meet the asking price for the Lexus SUV.

"Would you accept a certified bank check?" the buyer asked.

The victims couldn't believe their luck. Shortly after listing their vehicle for sale, they found a buyer with no uncomfortable haggling.

The next day, the man returned to close the deal. After examining the check, the victims handed the man keys and title to their vehicle. The check was deposited, and all was right with the world. Three days later, the bank was on the phone, informing them the check was bad. Realizing they had been scammed, the victims called the police to report their vehicle stolen.

"Is there anything else you can remember that will help us catch these guys?" I asked the middle-aged housewife from Milford, Connecticut.

"It seemed odd that his mechanic was chauffeuring him around in another Lexus RX 330," she replied.

"Anything else?"

"I don't know if I should say."

"Listen, if you want me to catch these guys, you have to tell me everything."

"They had breath."

"Excuse me?"

"Both men had bad breath," the woman repeated.

I laughed, prompting the woman to add, "No, they really did."

"Anything else?" my partner asked.

"They also wore too much cologne," she whispered.

On the ride back to the office, my partner and I laughed at the victim's reluctance to disclose the perpetrator's periodontal disease.

"What do you make of this?" my partner asked.

"I think we're on the trail of the Halitosis Hustlers," I laughed.

"You know it's going to be a nightmare to catch these guys," my partner said.

"What do you mean?" I asked.

"Vic, this case will drown you in paperwork. You have to subpoena phone records and go through Craigslist to get a lead on these guys," my partner explained.

"There's another way."

"Oh yeah, what's that?" my partner asked.

"I'm going to set a trap."

When I returned to my office, I posted a Lexus RX 330 for sale on Craigslist. I priced the vehicle ten percent above market value to discourage legitimate buyers from calling in. I listed the office hello phone as a contact number. A hello phone is a confidential telephone assigned to a detective squad.

Our hello phone sat on a small table in my lieutenant's office. I couldn't just barge in to check messages on the answering machine. I had to tap on his door like a teenager before entering. Now, all I had to do was sit back and wait for the phone to ring.

Patience is not one of my strong points. I started poking my head into the office every fifteen minutes to see if someone had left a message.

"Vic, you're going to wear out my floor if you keep coming in here," Chumley said.

Chumley and I had a love-hate relationship predicated on respect for the other's ability to get things done. I questioned authority, and he had to let me know he was in charge. Chumley needed me to produce arrests. I needed him to smooth things over after I rubbed countless supervisors the wrong way. Despite the unorthodox working relationship, we coexisted because we loved our work.

After four days of waiting, the hello phone rang.

"The hello phone! Quiet!" I shouted, racing across the office into Chumley's office.

I took a deep breath before picking up the phone, hoping my African con man was on the line.

"Hello," I said.

"Hi, do you have a Lexus RX 330 for sale?" the man asked.

He had an accent. But it was too early to tell. New York City is home to countless ethnic cultures.

"Yes, it's still for sale," I replied.

"I'd like to see it," the man said.

I set the sting for the following afternoon in the lobby of a six-story condominium on Henry Hudson Parkway. I told the friendly buyer I'd meet him in the lobby before bringing him to my underground garage to inspect the vehicle.

"Would you mind if I bring my mechanic along?" he asked as I tried to zero in on his accent. I tried to be fair and impartial, but in my heart, I knew this was the guy I was looking for.

"Sure, no problem," I said, trying not to sound like an anxious cop.

After giving him directions from Brooklyn, I added a caveat to the meeting.

"Listen, before you come out here, the price is firm at thirty-five thousand," I explained.

"That's not a problem," the man replied before saying goodbye.

"Ferrari, you got a lot of balls," Chumley laughed as I hung up the phone.

"Lou, I wanted to make sure it was him. Besides, he doesn't care how much it costs. He's going to pay with a phony check," I replied.

The following morning, I strapped a recording device the size of a pack of cigarettes underneath my armpit. Chumley called an office meeting where I mapped out escape routes and surveillance assignments.

The field team would arrive an hour before the meeting to secure vantage points around the building. I'd be waiting in the lobby, praying the battery-operated Kell (transmitter) didn't burn a hole in my armpit.

"What code word do you want to use?" Chumley asked.

"Code word?" I asked.

"Yeah, a code word to let us know when to move in," Chumley said.

"Mouthwash," I replied, causing the office to break out into laughter.

"Everyone hear that? We move in on mouthwash," Chumley instructed before we headed out to the location.

I got dropped off a few blocks from the building in case the Nigerian swindlers were conducting counter-surveillance. Once inside the empty lobby, I began admiring the endless rows of brass mailboxes beside the elevator.

Five minutes before the meeting, my Nextel phone chirped.

"Vic, they just pulled up in a white Lexus SUV with a temporary plate," Chumley said.

"Lou, it's probably stolen. We might as well take them now," I replied.

"Mouthwash! I mean, move in!" Chumley shouted into his portable radio.

I ran out of the building as my field team escorted two well-dressed men out of a stolen Lexus SUV. Inside their vehicle was a briefcase containing fraudulent bank checks and a business card from Mohammed Motors.

"I've been looking for you guys," I said, leading them to my unmarked car.

On the ride back to my office, the brains of the operation began asking questions.

"Why did you arrest us? We have done nothing wrong," he said, unleashing a poisonous dose of dragon breath.

"We'll talk about that when we get to my office," I explained.

"I'm not talking to you. I want a lawyer," he said.

"Sure, I'll get you a lawyer," I replied.

"And a dentist," my partner shouted, rolling down the windows to air out the vehicle.

The Nigerian con men were picked out of multiple lineups, confirming their roles in the well-planned scam. After posting bail, they fled the country and were never heard from again. Mohammed was sentenced to probation and ordered to pay restitution to the man who had spent the weekend in jail.

"I didn't think you believed me," the wrongly accused man said after I told him the good news.

"I didn't. I had to hear the other sides of the story," I explained.

"My word wasn't good enough?"

"Listen, had I taken Mohammad's word at face value, you'd still be in jail."

"Two sides to every story?" he asked.

"Three," I explained.

I think back to how uneventful the takedown was. The two scam artists pulling up in a stolen Lexus ruined my Donnie Brasco debut. At one point, it felt like the hair under my armpit had caught fire from the radioactive box taped to my body. Bad breath, reluctant victims, and misleading Mohammed made an interesting case. No matter how something looks, there are three sides to every story.

NINETY-SIX-HOUR PERMIT

Everyone lies to the police. I got lied to so often during my NYPD career that I'd ask my priest to repeat the sermon to ensure he wasn't trying to put one over on me. People will say anything to get out of a ticket or go to jail. I understand the mindset because, as a teenager, I lied to the cops every time they pulled me over.

When the officer got out of his patrol car, I started making up stories and begging for forgiveness. Sometimes it worked, sometimes it didn't, so I tried not to take it personally when I got hit with a bullshit story.

In the early nineties, auto theft was a booming business. New York City averaged a hundred and fifty thousand stolen vehicles a year. There were so many stolen vehicles buzzing around that it was nothing to see a car missing a hood or fender drive by on its way to a scrap metal processor. Cars get stolen for various reasons, but most of the time, it is for their parts. Back then, stolen auto parts were bought and sold in mob-controlled salvage yards across New York City's five boroughs. The black market for this commodity is a thriving business.

It was about to get more lucrative when the federal government mandated airbags in new vehicles. Overnight, they became a hot ticket item for every car thief and road pirate looking to make a quick buck. Thieves usually get five hundred dollars for a set of airbags while the body shop or junkyard sells them back to the unsuspecting victims for triple the price.

It got so bad that car dealerships would lose twenty sets of airbags at a time while thieves carrying duffle bags walked into salvage yards the following morning.

One winter afternoon, while patrolling the Gun Hill Road section of the Bronx, my partner and I decided to grab a coffee at the local McDonald's.

While waiting at the drive-through, a late model Nissan Maxima with temporary tags cruised through the parking lot.

"Holy shit, that Maxima is missing its airbags," my partner said.

"Let's check it out," I replied, pulling out of the drive-through after the suspicious vehicle.

The Maxima pulled into a parking space while I pulled behind its rear bumper.

"Do me a favor and please remain in the car," I instructed the occupants over the PA system.

While walking up to the vehicle, I observed two nervous men rummaging through the center console.

"What happened to your airbags?" I asked, pointing to the two large voids in the dashboard.

"Oh, I got it like this," the driver replied.

"Who's car is this?"

"It belongs to the dealership," he explained while handing me his driver's license and an envelope filled with paperwork.

"What dealership?"

"Oh, it's in South Carolina."

"Why do you have a car from a South Carolina car dealership?"

"I'm taking it for a test ride," he replied.

"A car dealership in South Carolina gave you a car to test drive in the Bronx?" I asked.

"Yeah, they gave me a ninety-six-hour permit," the driver explained, pointing to the paperwork.

No car dealership trusts a potential customer with a vehicle for four days. Even if the fugazy-looking documents were real, this guy was on borrowed time.

"This permit expires at six o'clock tonight," I said, examining the photocopied paperwork.

"So?" the driver asked.

"Well, you're going to have to drive fast to get this car back to South Carolina by six p.m.," I laughed.

On the other side of the car, I could hear my partner snickering as the driver continued to push his ridiculous story.

"Give me a few minutes," I said, returning to the radio car with his paperwork.

"There's no fucking way this car is legit," my partner said while running the Nissan's vehicle identification number in our mobile computer terminal.

I had heard many bullshit stories, but this one belonged in the Hall of Fame. There were more holes in this guy's story than the dashboard of his car.

"How can this be?" my partner asked, staring at the computer screen in disbelief.

"What's up?" I asked.

"The car isn't reported stolen."

"Watch these guys," I said, grabbing the paperwork off the dashboard.

"Where are you going?" my partner asked.

"I'm calling the dealership to sort this out," I replied.

Inside the restaurant, I asked the McDonald's manager if I could use his telephone.

"Is it a local call?" he asked.

"Yes," I replied.

I realize cops shouldn't lie. But I wasn't under oath or signing a sworn statement. Before cell phones and unlimited minutes, patrol cops had to get creative to access information.

The manager led me into a small office filled with 1970s McDonald's memorabilia. Dialing the South Carolina car dealership, I felt I was being watched. Looming above me were vintage posters of Grimace, The Hamburglar, and Mayor McCheese.

"I got two clowns up here in the Bronx with one of your cars, and I think it might be stolen," I explained to the receptionist.

"Hold on, I'm going to look for the owner," she replied before placing me on hold. While listening to mind-numbing muzak, I noticed the McDonald's manager was keeping tabs on me from a supply closet across the hall.

"Bronx, New York?" a gruff man's voice said into the phone.

"There's only one. Are you the owner of the dealership?" I asked.

"I'm the owner, all right. I understand you have one of my cars up there."

"I do. It's a brand-new Maxima with a little over eight hundred miles on it."

"If it has eight hundred miles on it, it's not a new car."

I gave him the vehicle identification number and asked if it was missing from his lot.

"Hold on. I have to do a lot count," he replied before putting me on hold.

The muzak wasn't better the second time, prompting the creepy McDonald's manager to begin pacing outside the office.

After fifteen minutes of waiting, I had an answer. "Yup, that's my car, and it's missing," the owner replied.

"These guys have a set of keys and photocopied paperwork from your dealership. Where do you think they got it from?"

"How the hell should I know? I just own the place. If I had to guess, it's probably from one of my disgruntled employees."

"I'm guessing you'd like to press charges?"

"Hell yeah. Lock them up and throw away the key. What kind of shape is my car in?" the owner asked.

"Other than the missing airbags, it's in pretty good shape."

"Sons of bitches, picking at my vehicle like a pack of vultures," the owner complained.

"Let me ask you, what's the story with these ninety-six-hour permits? I asked.

"What the fuck is a ninety-six-hour permit?" the owner replied.

"Never mind. Let me get the ball rolling with these arrests. I'll get you back in a few days and let you know when you can pick up your car."

After I hung up, the voyeuristic McDonald's manager entered the office.

"South Carolina?" he asked.

I didn't know how long he'd been listening to my conversation, but it was long enough to know I had placed a long-distance call.

"Yeah, I'm sorry about that. The investigation went south of the Mason-Dixon line," I laughed.

"The owner of this franchise watches every penny," the McDonald's manager said.

"How much do I owe you for the call?" I asked, reaching into my pocket.

"How about a PBA card?" the manager asked.

Everyone in New York City wants a Patrolmen's Benevolent Association card. Theoretically, the coveted courtesy card can get you out of a traffic ticket. In reality, it's up to the cop who pulled you over. Every NYPD cop is hounded for PBA cards. You only get four a year; the rest you must pay for. I only gave them to my parents and a few close friends during my NYPD career.

Before returning to the parking lot, I begrudgingly promised the McDonald's manager a PBA card. The ability to get out of a traffic ticket trumped the cost of a long-distance phone call. Despite their pleas of innocence, I arrested the pair for the stolen Maxima. We probably wouldn't have noticed them if they had not pulled the airbags out of the dashboard. Their ridiculous story of a ninety-six-hour road test up the Eastern Seaboard would not hold up in court. Ninety-six hours is a long time to trust anyone with anything, especially a new car.

A few days after the arrests, I got a call from my new friend in South Carolina.

"I appreciate you getting my car back," the owner of the Nissan dealership said.

"No problem," I replied.

"If you're ever in South Carolina, stop by the dealership. I can get you a great deal on a new Nissan."

"I appreciate the offer, but my department forbids me from accepting gratuities or discounts," I explained.

"Oh, that's too bad. But I'd like to thank you somehow."

"That's not necessary," I explained.

"Fair enough," he said.

As I was about to say goodbye, the car dealer had one last question.

"Would it be too much trouble if I could get one of those PBA cards?"

THE WAKE-UP CALL

Working for the New York City Police Department is more of a lifestyle than a career. It can be a real wake-up call when you realize you're no longer in control of your destiny. For the next twenty years, the department is running your life.

When you're a rookie cop, you do as you're told. You don't question the hours or assignments. Mandatory overtime, assignment changes, and acts of God have ruined many NYPD members' plans. There's just too much going on in New York City to enjoy a stable lifestyle.

The average American works Monday to Friday, nine to five, and enjoys the weekends and holidays off. NYPD members work around the clock and are lucky when they can go home on time.

When you need a day off, it's not going to happen. Need to leave work early? Sorry, we're at minimum manning. And you can forget spending Thanksgiving, Christmas, New Year's Eve, and the Fourth of July with your loved ones.

Sadly, I watched several talented detectives throw away promising careers because they felt slighted by the department. One guy never got over being ordered to work the dreaded New Year's Eve detail in Times Square. From that day forward, he was a bitter son of a bitch, hellbent on getting back at the department. The problem was he screwed everyone in our office to accomplish his goal.

You'll live a happier life if you go with the flow instead of trying to even the score. Working in a super competitive place like the NYPD's Auto Crime Division was no different.

One morning, while I was sipping coffee at my desk, the phone rang. Before I could answer, my officemate Jerry swooped in like a vulture and almost pulled the phone receiver from my hand.

"I got it," he smirked.

That was fine by me. I had a terrible headache and didn't want to talk to anyone. The day before, I and three other geniuses from my office drove ninety miles into Connecticut to win big at Mohegan Sun Indian gaming casino. Unfortunately, the only thing we came back with were empty pockets and hangovers. After a night of partying, the four broke-ass detectives decided to tough it out and return to work the following day. There's no honor among thieves or NYPD detectives. The pact dissolved the moment all parties reached a telephone. When I called our main office in Queens to ask for the day off, the duty sergeant laughed.

"What's going on in the Bronx office?" he asked.

"What do you mean?" I replied.

"There must be a blue flu going around because, in the last fifteen minutes, your partner, Murphy, and Johnson all called begging for tomorrow off," he laughed.

"I guess I'm out of luck," I replied.

"You guessed correctly," the sergeant said.

"Those dirty bastards, they screwed me," I complained.

Groggy from the night before, I attempted to eavesdrop on my coworker's telephone conversation. From what I could gather, the caller was ratting out an acquaintance who stole a car and stashed it in the Parkchester section of the Bronx. After Jerry got off the phone, he said, "I just got the strangest phone call."

"What's up?" I asked.

Jerry explained the anonymous caller was a jilted lover with an ax to grind. "His boyfriend sneaks into the coat rooms of Manhattan dance clubs."

"So?" I replied.

"He combs through patrons' coat pockets and steals their keys. Then, he walks around the neighborhood pushing key fobs until he can open a car."

"That's a new way to steal a car."

"Last night, he stole a new Mitsubishi Galant and stashed it on Thieriot Avenue."

"Do you have the license plate number?" I asked.

"I do," Jerry smiled.

"That's pretty specific information. I'll bet your anonymous caller is a jilted lover who went along for the ride."

"Oh, definitely, but I don't give a shit why he's ratting him out. A collar is a collar. I'll take what I can get," Jerry laughed.

"Before you go on a wild goose chase, run the plate to make sure the car was reported stolen," I said.

Jerry disappeared into the computer room to run the license plate while I poked through some paperwork on my desk. Within seconds, he returned with a shit-eating grin.

"So far, so good," he said, holding a stolen vehicle printout.

"Look, Vic, I know you're banged up from last night, but would you mind taking a ride with Tony and me to check this out?" Jerry asked, rolling his eyes at his overweight partner, whose face was buried in the morning newspaper. Another thing most NYPD members have no control over is who they work with.

Our lieutenant managed our office like a poorly run fantasy football league. He had a habit of pairing detectives who despised each other. In his infinite wisdom, Chumley arranged more dysfunctional marriages than Warren Jeffs. When Jerry was assigned to our office, Chumley paired him with the lazy Tony, hoping it would motivate him.

The problem was nothing motivated Tony. He was a bottom feeder who piggybacked on other detectives' cases to grab a few low-level arrests to justify his existence.

Tony's mantra, "I'll take a collar," said it all. He'd take an arrest if it was handed to him but never did the work himself.

Despite my hangover, Jerry figured I'd have more energy than his lazy partner. I went to work that morning hoping to catch up on paperwork, not sit on a stolen vehicle.

But, as I mentioned earlier, you can never plan your day as a member of the New York City Police Department, so I agreed to go along for the ride.

Jerry grabbed a set of keys for an unmarked car while Tony scooped up a couple of portable radios.

"Hey, Vic, do you mind if I ride in the back seat?" Tony asked, already looking like he wanted to take a nap.

"Come on, Tony, Jerry's your partner. I'm the third wheel."

Just as we were about to head out, Chumley came out of his office.

"Why is it necessary for three detectives to investigate this tip?" he asked.

"Lou, my partner, took the day off, so I figured I would go along for the ride," I explained.

"What is today? A national holiday? Half the office took the day off. What if something comes up, or I need somebody to grab me a sandwich?"

Chumley kept the office guessing with his twisted logic. Not wanting to piss him off, I returned to my desk.

"Screw it, go ahead. Keep your radio on in case I need you," Chumley instructed.

On our ride to Parkchester, Jerry asked, "Why does that old bastard give a shit if the three of us go out on this?"

"He's lonely and doesn't want to get stuck in the office alone," I replied.

"Lonely? He's been on the job for over thirty years. His kids are grown, and he doesn't have a mortgage. Why the fuck doesn't he retire already?"

"Because his wife doesn't want him home."

"So you feel bad for him?"

"Yeah, I kinda do."

"Not bad enough to hang around the office all day listening to his crazy theories?" Jerry asked.

"No, Jerry," I laughed.

He had me there. Chumley wasn't a bad guy, but he could be a royal pain in the ass. His domineering personality and the need to be right all the time made him a strong cup of coffee. Despite all his quirks, the salty Irishman wasn't the worst person to work for. While Jerry and I complained about the injustices of our office, lazy Tony had an epiphany.

"Are you guys hungry?" he asked.

"Jesus, Tony, it's not even ten o'clock, and we haven't found our stolen car yet," Jerry said.

With food on his mind twenty-four hours a day, Tony planned his work schedule around restaurant locations. The big-boned, olive-skinned oaf resembled a calzone with legs.

Fat Tony was notorious for devouring leftovers in the office refrigerator. Anything sitting in Tupperware or a styrofoam container was fair game. It didn't matter how bad it smelled or how long it was there for. Tony was a junkyard dog that could eat off the floor without getting a stomach ache.

Searching for the stolen Mitsubishi Galant in the north end of the Forty-Third Precinct meant slim pickings for the human garbage can. After promising Tony we'd find him something to eat, we cruised around the Parkchester neighborhood in search of the stolen vehicle.

Thieriot Avenue was lined with six-story graffiti-riddled buildings that had seen better days. The once working-class Irish neighborhood was now awash in poverty and drugs. Open fire hydrants spilled into the gutter along piles of uncollected garbage. As we rolled down Thieriot Avenue, I spotted the stolen Mitsubishi.

"Thar she blows," I shouted, pointing to the silver sedan.

Jerry drove to the end of the block and dropped me off to inspect the stolen vehicle. At ten a.m., Thieriot Avenue was a ghost town. No one noticed as I approached the silver Mitsubishi Galant and copied its vehicle identification number before returning to our unmarked car.

"Well?" Tony asked.

"It's a match," I replied.

We set up an observation post on the corner of Theriot and East Tremont Avenue. There, we could monitor the stolen Galant without being seen.

During my NYPD career, I learned several valuable lessons on how to sit on a stolen vehicle. If you park too close, the vehicle is going to get burned. The neighborhood street urchins will notice you, and no one will get in the car again.

If you park too far away, something will obstruct your vision, and the car will drive off without you noticing. To avoid these pitfalls, you have to find the right distance to monitor the vehicle without drawing attention to yourself.

After twenty minutes of surveillance, Tony began complaining about his empty stomach.

"You guys aren't hungry?" he whined.

"Tony, we just got here. Give it a little time to develop before we leave to get something to eat," Jerry said.

"Jerry, I didn't eat breakfast," Tony complained.

"What if the car leaves while we're gone?" Jerry asked.

"Jerry, whoever stole the car isn't awake yet. Let me make a quick run to Wendy's. I'll be back in ten minutes," Tony said.

"You expect Vic and me to stand on the corner waiting for this clown to get into a stolen car while you're grabbing a snack? Jerry asked.

Ignoring his partner's response, Tony started badgering me, "Vic, you're hungry, right?"

"Jerry is right. Give it some time," I replied.

"You guys don't understand. I didn't eat breakfast," Tony pleaded, like his life depended on a Wendy's combo.

"Oh my God, I can't take it," Jerry shouted.

"Come on, Jerry, I'll get you one of those stuffed potatoes you like," Tony said.

After several minutes of intense negotiations, Jerry cracked and handed Tony the keys.

"Get your ass back here in ten minutes," Jerry reminded his partner like a parent enforcing a curfew.

While fat Tony raced down East Tremont Avenue in search of angina, Jerry and I watched the stolen car from a block away.

"Your partner is a selfish fuck," I said.

"You're not telling me anything I don't know," Jerry replied.

"How long do you want to spend sitting on this car?" I asked.

"Why?" Jerry asked.

"Because three hours from now, when Tony is hungry, I'm not standing out here again," I replied.

"What do you suggest?" Jerry asked.

"I got an idea," I said, pointing to a bodega across the street.

Jerry and I walked into the neighborhood grocery and purchased a dozen eggs. Pulling our hoodies over our heads, we raced past the stolen car and pelted it with a handful of grade A's. No one noticed the two hooded miscreants sprinting back to their vantage point on E Tremont Avenue.

"I haven't done that since I was a kid," Jerry laughed.

"That should motivate our thief to bring it to a car wash," I replied.

While Jerry and I were busy laughing at the childhood prank, the hazard lights on the stolen Mitsubishi Galant blinked.

"Someone just deactivated the alarm," Jerry said.

Within minutes, a tall, well-built man wearing a canary fleece came trotting out of a building towards the vehicle.

"Let's start walking. We'll charge him once he gets into the car," I said.

While Jerry and I made our way down Thieriot Avenue, the canary fleece was busy inspecting his stolen vehicle. He seemed annoyed, flicking pieces of eggshells off the car while running his fingers across the roof like a *Price is Right* model.

I approached on the sidewalk while Jerry paralleled from the street. About halfway down the block, the yellow fleece opened the driver's door and climbed inside the stolen vehicle. Jerry and I took off running as the Mitsubishi Galant came to life.

I pulled open the passenger door and shouted, "Police, get out of the car!"

Startled, the driver slammed the car in reverse, ramming the car behind him. Jerry pulled open the driver's door and grappled with him. I reached into the vehicle and pulled the key from the ignition.

"You got nowhere to go, pal," I yelled, attempting to push him out of the car.

"Jesus, Vic, this guy is strong as an ox," Jerry shouted, pulling on the stylish thief's arm. I ran around to the other side of the vehicle and started pulling his other arm.

"Let go of the steering wheel," Jerry shouted as sweat rolled down his face. Without warning, the beefy twenty-something car thief let go of the steering wheel and lunged out of the vehicle, knocking Jerry and me to the ground.

"Grab his legs," I shouted as the three of us rolled across the unforgiving pavement. Jerry wrapped his arms around the thief's legs while I attempted to slap a handcuff on his wrist. It was obvious we were no match for the hulking suspect as we struggled to get him under control. After several minutes of fighting, Jerry and I wore down.

"I can't hold him much longer," Jerry screamed, his head buried in the perp's thigh.

With one handcuff dangling off his wrist, I attempted to pull the other arm behind his back.

"Vic, forget that! Call a thirteen! (10-13 officer needs assistance code)," Jerry yelled.

I reached into my back pocket and couldn't find my radio.

"Oh shit," I yelled.

My eyes darted along the pavement, searching for the missing Motorola radio. It must have dropped out of my pocket when we were playing Twister on the ground. When I lifted my head, I discovered the once barren Thieriot Avenue had come to life. A small crowd had gathered around the brawl and appeared to be taking bets on its outcome. Crowds are unpredictable. All you need is one rabble-rouser, and this could get ugly fast. For now, the pack seemed more curious than hostile, watching Jerry and I trade blows with the perp. That could change at any moment, so we had to wrap this up fast.

"Somebody call the police," I shouted, hoping to motivate someone in the crowd to call 911.

No one blinked, meaning Jerry and I were on our own. After pleading with the curious crowd, I spotted my portable radio several feet away underneath the stolen Galant.

"Jerry, can you hold on to him for a few seconds while I grab the radio?" I shouted.

"Yeah, fucking hurry!" he screamed.

I let go of the perp's arms and dove for the radio. After snatching it from beneath the car, I raised it to my mouth and shouted, "Ten thirteen! Theriot and Tremont, ten thirteen!" I shoved it back into my rear pocket.

The radio came to life with a symphony of police cars from the Forty-Third Precinct answering my call for help. "Forty-

Three David is going. Forty-Three Charley is going," and every cop in the Eighth Division was on their way.

"Back up!" I shouted at several voyeurs, who had moved in for a better look.

The violent struggle continued until sirens were heard in the distance.

"Now would be a good time to quit," Jerry shouted at the now compliant perp, who had stopped fighting. Eventually, we got him handcuffed before rising to our feet.

"Can I get up too?" the perp asked.

"Just stay there for now," I said, attempting to catch my breath.

"You okay?" Jerry asked.

"Yeah, I think I cut myself," I said, noticing blood on my hands and jacket.

"I got blood all over me too," Jerry said, looking over his clothing.

While Jerry and I tried to figure out where all the blood came from, the cavalry arrived from every angle.

"Auto Crime Portable, slow it down on Theriot Avenue," I said into my portable radio.

"Where is that fat fuck?" Jerry said, scanning through the crowd of cops for his partner.

While I explained what transpired to the Forty-Third patrol supervisor, our unmarked Buick Century rounded the corner on two tires. Late to the party with a carload of fast-food fat, Tony slammed on the brakes inches from the perp's body.

"Jesus, Tony, you almost ran over our collar's head," I said as he dragged his fat ass out of the car.

"I got here as fast as I could," Tony explained.

"Wait, you guys were out here without a car?" the sergeant asked with a tone of surprise.

"Yeah, kinda," I replied.

"May I ask why?" the sergeant queried.

"Sarge, look at the size of him. He can't go fifteen minutes without eating," I laughed and pointed at Tony.

"Well, by the looks of things, you guys are banged up. I suggest you go to Jacobi (hospital) and get checked out," the sergeant instructed.

Jerry and I grabbed the handcuffed perp under each arm and lifted him off the pavement. His bright canary fleece looked like a blood splattered Jackson Pollock abstract.

While escorting the perp to our unmarked car, he said, "I need to talk to you guys."

"After we're done at the hospital, I'll read you your Miranda warnings, and you can talk all you want," Jerry replied.

While shoving him into the backseat I noticed a nasty gash above his right eye.

"I need to tell you something. It's very important," the car thief said.

"Okay, what do you want to tell us?" I asked.

"I'm HIV positive," he said, hanging his head in his lap.

From the driver's seat, Jerry spun around and shouted, "Are you fucking kidding me?"

"I'm sorry," the perp replied.

"Jerry, get to Jacobi. Fast," I said, trying to snap him back into reality.

Just as we were about to drive off, Tony pulled alongside our car in the stolen Galant. "Hey, Jerry, toss me a burger?" he shouted out the window.

As shaken as I was, I had to laugh. Jerry and I were covered in HIV blood, and Tony wants a hamburger.

"You want a hamburger, you fat piece of shit? Here's your fucking hamburger!" Jerry shouted, firing the oil-stained paper bag at Tony's head.

"Jesus Christ, what's wrong?" Tony asked.

"Follow us to Jacobi," I shouted out the back window.

While Jerry raced us to the hospital, I talked to the prisoner.

"How long have you known you have HIV?" I asked.

"Two years," he replied.

"Are you taking medication for it?" I asked.

"Several," he sobbed.

"What's wrong?" I said.

"I don't want to go back to jail," he said.

"Come on. It's the Bronx. Nobody goes to jail for stealing a car in the Bronx," I replied, causing him to laugh.

"I'm sorry. I was scared and just wanted to get away," the prisoner explained.

"Well, I appreciate you telling us you're HIV positive," I replied.

When we reached the hospital, Tony watched the prisoner while Jerry and I raced into the emergency room.

"Where's the nearest bathroom?" I asked a nurse, who pointed to a room down the corridor. After kicking in the door, Jerry and I squeezed into the tiny bathroom. It was more a broom closet with a toilet and sink, but it would have to do to wash this blood off our hands.

"Hospital soap. This is the good stuff," Jerry explained, slamming his hand repeatedly into the front of the plastic soap dispenser.

"This fucking water is a million degrees," I shouted as scalding water dissolved the dried blood off my fingers and into the sink. Jerry and I lathered, rinsed, and repeated like Lady Macbeth for twenty minutes, hoping to avert a catastrophe. It seemed like blood was everywhere, hiding in every nook and cranny of our bodies.

"You got cuts or open wounds?" I asked, examining my hands and arms.

"I can't tell. But I look like a fucking burn victim," Jerry quipped, blowing on his red pruned fingers.

While Jerry and I searched for lacerations, Tony strolled by with the prisoner.

"Who is taking the collar?" Tony asked.

"I am," Jerry replied.

"But Jerry, I don't have a collar this month," Tony said.

"Whose fault is that?" Jerry snapped back.

"I've been in court all month," Tony reasoned.

"You've been in a deli all month," Jerry shouted, causing the prisoner to laugh.

"Jerry, I need to get on the sheet," Tony begged.

"Vic, you believe this fucking guy?" Jerry said.

"Tony, I hope you're kidding," I said.

This was classic Tony: showing up after the work was done and expecting a piece of the pie. Unfortunately for him, Jerry and I weren't about to let that happen.

"You motherfucker, this is all your fault!" Jerry shouted.

"My fault? How do you figure that?" Tony asked.

"If you hadn't left, we could have boxed him with the car in, and this wouldn't have happened," Jerry said, pointing to the blood on his clothing.

"Jerry, I was gone for five minutes," Tony whined.

"You had to stuff your fat face. Now Vic and I are covered in AIDS blood," Jerry complained.

"But, Jerry," Tony pleaded.

"Fuck you, Tony. I'm taking the collar," Jerry said before walking off.

Tony looked at me and raised his hands, hoping I'd sympathize with him.

"Tony, I don't know what to tell you," I said, following Jerry into the waiting room.

"You believe that fucking jabroni?" Jerry asked.

"I can't figure out if he's selfish or stupid," I replied.

"Both!" he shouted.

Jerry and I shared a laugh before the conversation turned to the dangers of exposure to HIV blood.

"God forbid, we get AIDS. There's no cure for that," Jerry said.

"No, there's not. But look at Magic Johnson. He's been HIV positive for a million years, and he's still going strong," I replied.

"I'll bet Magic Johnson's insurance provider is better than GHI," Jerry laughed.

"Can you imagine what our copays would be if we had access to his medical care?" I asked.

Cops will often default to humor in times of crisis. Worrying about our fates wouldn't change the outcome. There could be life-changing news on the horizon. We might as well laugh now while we have the opportunity. Having worked in the Narcotics Division, I was aware of the risks associated with HIV. Until this point in my career, I had never gotten jabbed with a needle or exposed to another person's blood.

After triage, Jerry and I were brought to a makeshift examination area. On the other side of the curtain was a man yelling in Spanish.

"Ay, dios mio!" he shouted.

"Mr. Sanchez, please hold still," the doctor instructed.

"Are they operating on this guy?" Jerry asked.

"Conyo!" the man screamed.

"Mr. Sanchez, you must hold still, or the needle could break in your spine," the doctor warned.

You never know what you'll find in a Bronx emergency room. Everything from gunshot wounds to spinal taps is on display in a germ-filled petri dish of humanity. While attempting to ignore the chaos in the next bay, a doctor poked his head through the curtain.

"Mind if I come in?" the young resident asked.

"Sure, come on in, Doc," I replied.

After looking at our charts, he asked, "Aside from the bumps and bruises, do you have any concerns?"

"Concerns? We just had a bare-knuckle brawl with an HIV-positive bodybuilder," I replied.

"I see. Well, let's take a look at you guys," the doctor said, placing his clipboard on the workstation.

After examining us from head to toe, he gave his diagnosis.

"As far as I can see, there is some swelling and bruising but no open wounds. Chances are you didn't get infected," the doctor said.

"Chances are?" Jerry asked.

"Detective, nothing is a hundred percent," the doctor replied.

"So, what are our options?" I asked.

"As you know, there have been major advances in the treatment of HIV. Some patients have lived over thirty years with the disease," the doctor explained.

"Major medical advances? We just listened to the Spanish Inquisition in the next cubicle," Jerry mocked.

"Oh, you heard that? Yeah, spinal taps can be tricky," the doctor admitted.

"Go on, Doc," Jerry said.

"If we were to proceed with treatment, I would start you on a cocktail of medications for three months," the doctor explained.

"So you're saying this treatment will prevent us from getting HIV?" I asked.

"It's possible but uncertain," the doctor explained.

"Is there a downside to the treatment?" I asked.

"There are always risks associated with medications. You'd be taking several powerful inhibitors and antiviral agents for several months," the doctor replied.

"What are the risks?" I asked.

"The treatment could damage your liver and kidneys," the doctor replied.

"That sounds risky," Jerry said.

"Well, you're dropping a nuke on your body, hoping to stop the disease before it can inhibit you," the doctor explained.

"What are the odds we were infected?" I asked.

"I've examined you both. Neither of you appear to have open wounds," the doctor said.

"And?" Jerry pressed.

"You guys have a decision to make," the doctor answered.

"What would you do?" I asked.

"If it were me? I'd forgo the treatment and get tested every six months for the next two years. It's an experimental treatment and far from a sure thing. I'll give you guys a couple of minutes to decide," the doctor said before disappearing through the curtain.

"What are you going to do, Vic?" Jerry asked.

"I'm ninety-nine percent sure I don't have any tears in my skin. I don't think the treatment is worth it," I replied.

"I was thinking the same thing," Jerry replied.

Jerry and I left the hospital with two packets of ibuprofen and lots of uncertainty. After changing our clothing, we processed the arrest and sent Fat Tony to the Whitestone pound to drop off the vehicle. The body building car thief had other problems besides his arrest for the stolen Mitsubishi. He was wanted by the Secret Service for credit card fraud and identity theft.

Fat Tony ate his way out of the Auto Crime Division a few months later. This time, he abandoned his post to grab a veal parmigiana sandwich while surveilling an organized crime figure.

"We're following a guy that killed ten people, and you left to get a sandwich?" our lieutenant asked before shipping Fat Tony off to the Narcotics Division.

The next two years were tough for Jerry and me. Having your blood drawn at a city clinic every six months is not as glamorous as it sounds. I never gave it much thought until I had a test. Then, it was two weeks of hell waiting for the results. After two years of testing negative, Jerry and I were clear. We no longer had to worry about HIV or AIDS. What should have been a peaceful day of paperwork escalated into a vicious street fight, followed by years of anxiety from exposure to a deadly disease. From that day forward, I realized I wasn't immortal, and the clock began to tick on my NYPD career. Six months after I got a clean bill of health, I put in my papers to retire from the New York City Police Department. All these years later, I have mixed emotions about retiring after my twentieth year.

Did I make the right decision? Should I have worked another couple of years, hoping to get promoted? Then I think back to that day, rolling around in the street covered in blood before waiting two years to learn my fate. That day was the wake-up call I needed to bring an end to my NYPD career. I hope my stories about auto theft help you hold on to your car. Remember, some thieves can steal your car with a pen just as easily with a screwdriver.

CHAPTER 8

THE MOUNTED UNIT

The NYPD's mounted unit dates back to 1858. Long before Henry Ford's Model T rolled off the assembly line, NYPD-mounted cops were patrolling New York City streets. The noble unit has provided safety to New Yorkers for over hundred fifty years and is a throwback in time. Let's start with the uniform. Unlike the standard NYPD patrolman's uniform (navy blue slacks, patent leather shoes, and iconic eight-point hat), mounted cops wear a helmet, riding pants, and a three-quarter-length leather jacket. Instead of a radio car, you get a horse.

Where do the horses come from? Well, NYPD horses aren't Arabian stallions or thoroughbred racehorses. They're bred by Amish horse breeders in Lancaster, Pennsylvania. Leave it to the NYPD to get their horses from a subculture who shun the automobile. Over the years, cops on horseback took a back seat to the patrol car. That doesn't mean they don't serve a purpose. Mounted cops are front and center at every parade and sporting event. After winning the 1996 World Series, Yankee third baseman Wade Boggs jumped on the back of a NYPD mounted cop's horse for a victory lap around Yankee stadium. When the shit hits the fan, no one is better at controlling a crowd than the mounted unit. When that horse turns sideways, people get knocked on their ass. Mounted cops are out in all kinds of weather and essential to keeping rowdy drunks in line at the New Year's Eve celebration in Times Square.

Navigating through a crowded city on a two-thousand-pound animal can be dangerous. Mounted cops are often injured when kicked or thrown from their horses.

In the early eighties, a mounted policeman got launched head-first into the pavement by his chestnut-colored stallion. While the cop lay unconscious, his trusty sidekick returned to the barn. A few hours later, panic set in when Seabiscuit was found meandering around the stables without its rider. A manhunt ensued for the missing cop until he was discovered on a Bronx street critically injured. He was rushed to the hospital for his injuries. Eventually, the cop pulled through and was awarded a disability pension for his injuries.

When my friend told me the story, I asked, "How is he doing?"

"You know," he said, shrugging his shoulders.

"What do you mean?" I asked.

"I worked with the guy for five years. Every time I run into him, I have to re-introduce myself."

A COP RIDES INTO A BAR ON A HORSE

NYPD mounted cops working in Midtown Manhattan live a charmed life. Like the Beefeaters guarding Buckingham Palace, equestrian cops are more for show until something falls into their lap. They spend their days providing tourists with directions and photo opportunities in front of New York City landmarks like the Empire State Building and Madison Square Garden. Everyone loves a cop on a horse, including the businesses that benefit from them standing in front of their establishments. Mounted cops attract more attention than any inflatable mannequin or sign spinner can muster. One such business was a local dive bar on the west side of Manhattan. In the mid-1970s, a mounted cop and his horse stopped daily at the neighborhood watering hole.

In the back of the old saloon was a small beer garden where the cop would tie up his horse before partaking in a liquid lunch.

The landmark bar had large double doors, providing enough width for the horse to walk through. The towering mounted cop would lower his head before entering as the horse strolled through the bar. Several times the horse crapped on the floor, sending drunks into the local OTB to place a wager.

"It's good luck," they'd convince themselves while rubbing the betting slips between their fingers.

The hard luck bar could have hosted a casting call for a revival of Eugene O'Neill's classic *The Iceman Cometh*.

While the mounted cop sipped his gin and tonics at the bar, patrons fed carrots to their four-legged friend out back. For years, the cop and horse show was the best-kept secret in the insular Irish enclave known as Hell's Kitchen. During this time, a gang of thugs known as the Westies terrorized the neighborhood, shaking down local businesses for protection money. No one dared call Internal Affairs on Wilbur and Ed, whose daily presence kept the gang at bay. One hot summer afternoon, the horse unexpectedly dropped dead in the garden, causing panic inside the bar.

The mounted cop had a major problem on his hands. How would he explain what his horse was doing in the back of a bar? The NYPD prohibits its members from consuming alcohol on duty. I'm also sure there are countless rules and regulations on where to park the horse during your meal hour that don't include a saloon. If the mounted cop called for help on his portable radio, that would raise many uncomfortable questions.

How would he get this dead horse out of the bar?

The bartender called his brother, who owned a local towing company. Minutes later, a banged-up wrecker arrived with a man holding a tape measure.

"Why did you tell me to bring a tape measure? I thought I was towing a car?" the tow truck driver asked.

The man followed his brother through the bar and out to the garden, where he found the sobbing mounted cop grieving beside his dead horse.

"Holy shit," the tow truck driver said.

"Can you pull him through the bar?" the bartender asked.

"How did he die?" the tow truck driver asked.

"I don't know. We didn't have time for an autopsy," the bartender mocked.

"Will you be able to get him out of here?" the mounted cop asked.

"If the cable can reach and the doors are wide enough, I should be able to pull him out of here," the tow truck driver replied.

The tow truck backed up to the front door while a steel cable was pulled through the bar and out to the garden.

"Hurry, we don't have all day," the bartender shouted at his brother, who attempted to hook the ring of the horse's bridle.

"Calm down. I've never towed a horse before," the tow truck driver replied.

"Well, try not to damage anything," the gin blossom bartender barked as the tow truck winch began reeling in the cable through the smoke-filled bar.

As the two-thousand-pound animal was dragged across the hardwood floor, a few patrons began singing "Danny Boy." With tears in his eyes, the bartender raised a glass of whiskey, saying goodbye to an old friend for the last time.

When the horse reached the sidewalk, the bereaved mounted cop sprang into action, calling for help on his portable radio. The tow truck driver knew better than to hang around and took off the minute he unhooked the cable.

When his supervisor arrived, the mounted cop gave an Academy-Award-winning performance. He explained through a river of tears how his beloved horse suddenly dropped dead in the street in front of the bar. Several sobbing drunks backed up the mounted cop's story. A few days later, the bar held a memorial service where neighborhood barflies paid their respects to a fallen comrade.

Eventually, the mounted cop returned to the bar with his new partner, a shiny filly named Mary Jane. Having learned his lesson, Mary Jane never stepped inside the Hell's Kitchen bar. Instead, she patiently waited outside, tied to a parking meter, while her partner socialized inside.

HORSESHIT

Owning an Irish Wolfhound is a tremendous responsibility. The giant breed requires more exercise than the average canine. My first Irish Wolfhound (Angelo) resembled an elk and ran like the wind. When I lived in the Bronx, I would take him for long walks around the neighborhood.

During one afternoon walk, I ran into my father.

"Do you ever let that thing off the leash?" my father asked.

"Of course, I do. Do you think I keep him chained up inside the house?" I replied.

"Have you ever taken him to the park to run around?"

I'd taken my hound to the dog park several times, which ended in catastrophe. Once, he knocked a woman on her ass. The other time, he mounted a Pekingese.

"I don't know if that's a good idea," I said.

"He's a big dog. He needs to run," my father instructed.

Taking my father's advice, I took my hound to Pelham Bay Park. The twenty-seven-hundred-acre park would provide plenty of room for my Irish Wolfhound to stretch his legs.

Walking towards an enormous field, I had second thoughts.

I wanted my dog to have a good time, but I was unsure how he would react to his newfound freedom. He had never been off the leash before. Would he come back when called? Or would he run into the woods, never to be seen again? I felt like a parent giving my teenage son the keys to the family vehicle for the first time.

"You had better come back when I call you," I instructed, slipping the collar off his furry neck.

Tilting his head, he stared into my eyes, not realizing he was a free man.

"Go ahead," I said, shooing him away.

He stared, wagging his tail, before I shouted, "Go!"

Suddenly, the light went on, and he took off across the open field.

Irish Wolfhounds don't run. They gallop. Like thoroughbred racehorses, they tear up the ground with their claws. As my dog raced by, I could see the dirt fly through his enormous paws. My hundred-twenty-pound wolfhound ran circles around me with unbridled enthusiasm. After several minutes of racing around, he stopped to examine an enormous pile of horseshit.

I didn't see that when I let him off the leash.

"Angelo, get over here," I shouted as he shoved his long snout into the mountain of crap.

Leash in hand, I took off running, hoping to retrieve my hound before it was too late. He picked up his head with a defiant stare before diving head first into a mountain of shit.

"Angelo, stop!" I pleaded.

My mind raced with emotion. What was I going to do? I had to get him on the leash before he did any more damage. He began rolling around in the dung as I closed in on my disobedient hound. As I went to slip the collar around his neck, he bent down and grabbed a mouthful for the ride home.

Why did I listen to my father? He never owned a dog weighing over ten pounds and never let them off the leash. Now my beautiful show dog was covered in shit.

Where do I go from here? I couldn't put him in my car like this, and it was too far to walk home. I began weighing my options while my hound paraded around, happy as a pig in shit. After wracking my brain, I had a moment of clarity. Where did all that horseshit come from? The NYPD's mounted unit.

I remembered they had riding stables at the back of Pelham Bay Park. One of their horses must have crapped in the field before moving on to greener pastures. They were responsible for this debacle.

"Come on, Angelo," I said, walking towards the restricted area. I followed a trail past a couple of horse trailers before making our way to a large compound with a sign that read: *NYPD Mounted Unit Troop D and No Trespassing.*

"Hello?" I shouted before entering the large barn filled with stables.

Growing up in the Bronx, I didn't know my way around a barn or farm animals. My uncle once owned a farm in upstate New York where Fredo and I were often injured. Once, a herd of cows almost trampled us for tossing crab apples in their direction. Attempting to escape the stampede, I burned my crotch climbing over an electric fence designed to keep the animals on the property.

I tiptoed through a minefield of hay and horseshit, trying my best not to ruin my sneakers. After tying Angelo's leash to an empty stable, I looked for a hose.

While passing a stable, a head popped up from behind a horse's ass and shouted, "Hey, this is a police facility. You can't be back here."

"I'm on the job," I said, handing the young cop in Doc Martens my police identification card.

"You still can't be back here."

"Listen, pal, my dog and I are covered in horseshit, and we're not leaving until we've cleaned up," I said, grabbing a garden hose.

"But the inspector doesn't want anyone back here," the nervous cop pleaded.

While I argued with Dudley Do-Right, a curious goat nudged me from behind. "What the fuck!" I shouted, jumping away.

"It's just a goat," the mounted cop explained.

"What the hell is it doing here?"

"He keeps the horses calm."

"What the hell do they have to worry about?"

"Listen, you really have to go."

"The faster you get me some shampoo, the faster we'll be out of your hair," I said.

Finally, the by-the-book stable hand walked to a locker and retrieved a large plastic jug of shampoo.

"Mane and tail horse shampoo?" I laughed, examining the label.

"Yeah, it's great stuff. Could you please hurry?" the mounted cop begged.

While I rinsed clumps of crap off my dog, the mounted cop watched for his supervisor.

"Where do you work?" he asked.

"The Auto Crime Division."

"That must be a fun place to work."

"It beats washing off horseshit," I replied.

FINAL PARADE

Speaking of horseshit, a few days before retiring from the New York City Police Department, I volunteered to work the Puerto Rican Day parade. The Sunday morning detail would be the last time I'd wear my NYPD uniform. A lot had changed during my twenty years with the department, including the uniform. When I was hired in 1987, our uniform shirt was powder blue. The iconic color was immediately recognizable, making the NYPD uniform stand out from other police departments. That changed in 1995 when some genius at One Police Plaza tinkered with the color scheme. From that day forward, a hot navy-blue polyester shirt made the NYPD indistinguishable from every police department in the county.

My partner and I grabbed a post along the parade route off East 57th Street. I was looking forward to an easy day of overtime watching my final parade glide down Fifth Avenue. My good friend Lieutenant Hennessey had retired a few years earlier, but the borough of Manhattan South had remained the same.

While my partner and I enjoyed the colorful parade, someone shouted: "Detectives, face the crowd!"

"What now?" my partner said, looking over his shoulder.

Charging across the street like a heat-seeking missile was a young deputy inspector. He looked about fifteen years old and was holding onto the top of his hat so it wouldn't fly off his head.

"Why are you two standing together? Who has this post?" the inspector shouted.

"I do," my partner replied.

"So, you are off post?" he asked, pointing at me.

"Yes, sir," I replied.

"Detective, where do you work?" he asked, pulling a notepad from his back pocket.

"Does his father know he's wearing his uniform?" my partner muttered under his breath, causing me to smile.

"Auto Crime Division," I said, holding back laughter.

"You think this is funny? We'll see how funny this is after I stick this in your ass," the inspector said, copying down my name and shield.

After the informative lecture, the little inspector ran off to fuck with someone else. I didn't care about the command discipline. I'd be retired when it reached my office.

"Hennessey must have opened a school down here after he retired," I laughed.

"Fuck this, let's take a break," my partner said, gesturing towards Central Park.

Walking down East 59th Street across from the Plaza Hotel, we spotted a line of hansom cabs along the park.

"For our wedding anniversary, I took my wife for a ride around Central Park," my partner said.

"Was it fun?" I asked.

"Fun? It was fucking expensive," my partner complained.

While my partner bitched about his carriage ride, a horse lifted its tail and took a shit in the street.

"That's disgusting," I said.

"You toss a piece of paper on the ground, and you'll get hit with an ECB (Environmental Control Board) summons. But that thing can crap in the street all day, and no one raises an eyebrow," my partner replied.

Seconds later, the hansom cab had a fare: four Japanese tourists and a fistful of yen. As the horse and buggy pulled off, a flock of pigeons descended into the dung.

"Oh my God, are they eating that?" I asked.

"Sure looks like it," my partner replied.

For twenty minutes, I watched nature take its course. The squadron of flying rats devoured the pile of horseshit. It was the perfect metaphor for my time spent in the borough of Manhattan South. Hennessey might be long gone, but his ghost still ruled that borough with an iron fist.

CHAPTER 9

OFF-DUTY CONDUCT

You're walking on eggshells during the probationary period of your NYPD career. Paranoia is part of the job because the department can fire you for anything. During my field training, two fellow rookie cops were terminated after troubling information emerged from their pasts. One had spent time in a drug rehabilitation center. The other was involved in a home invasion with her dirtbag husband. No cop worth his salt would trust their life with a former drug addict or bandit ripping off drug dealers. But the guidelines for conduct don't end there.

The fastest way to lose your job is to engage in conduct the department finds "unbecoming of a police officer." It's a blanket statement meant to cover the department's ass when they want to fire someone over an off-duty incident. Most of the time, it's when alcohol is involved.

Disagree with the neighbor, drama with the girlfriend, or a skirmish at the bar will land you on the unemployment line. During my time in the police academy, they warned us countless times to stay out of bars during our probationary period. "You can lead a horse to water, but you can't keep a moron out of a saloon," was my motto when I should have been keeping my head down.

While attending the police academy, a few classmates and I stopped at a Lower East Side bar after work. As we bonded over dinner and drinks, several off-duty police academy gym instructors approached our group. They were cordial, purchasing a couple of pitchers of beer for the table while flirting with the female police recruits.

For me, it was time to go. I had my fill and had to catch the last express bus up to the Bronx. I never gave the evening a second thought until a few weeks later, when the administration started pulling my classmates out of the classroom.

"What the hell is going on?" I asked one of my friends who had been interrogated.

"They're looking to hang anyone who partied with the instructors the other night," he replied.

Little did I know that after I left the bar, the instructors took the party to a swank Manhattan hotel. The impressionable recruits followed while the instructors ordered champagne up to the room.

While all parties were consenting adults, that didn't excuse violating NYPD policy. One of the female recruits involved in the festivities made the mistake of telling her girlfriend, who ratted everyone out. When it was all said and done, they bounced the instructors out of the police academy while the recruits were relieved of several vacation days. Looking back, everyone involved was lucky. They all got to keep their jobs. If that had happened today, all of them would have been fired. The story would be front page news, with reporters camped out on everyone's front lawn asking for comment. Can you imagine? Cops having sex and drinking alcohol off-duty?

You would think that after watching that unfold, I wouldn't leave my house until I was off probation. Unaffected by the blowback, I tempted fate and met up with friends the night before I graduated from the police academy. The Green Leaf Bar in the Bronx was the perfect venue to celebrate. The Manhattan college bar featured a large dance floor and new wave music.

That night, the music was pumping as ice-cold long necks of beer flowed down my throat. My friends and I were having a grand old time, shouting over the sounds of Depeche Mode and inhaling secondary smoke, when a fight broke out in the back of the bar.

Whoever started the brawl was strong as an ox, tossing grown men to the floor like children. After a few people got knocked unconscious, the bouncers got their hands on the guy causing all the trouble. It looked like a tornado of bodies spinning in circles as they dragged the barroom brawler through the packed bar. On his way out the door, the strapping construction worker kicked and punched anyone he could get his hands on, igniting a full-blown donnybrook that spilled into the street. It looked like the fight scene in *The Quiet Man* with drunken men spitting out teeth.

To quell the riot, bartenders grabbed wooden hurling sticks from behind the bar and raced outside. It got so bad that the DJ abandoned his turntable to get his licks in.

"What are we supposed to do?" my friend asked, looking out the window at the chaos outside.

"I'm not going out there," I replied.

"Aren't you supposed to keep the peace?" my friend laughed.

"I'd like to keep my teeth," I said.

Trapped inside the vacant pub, I shrugged my shoulders and walked behind the bar.

"What are you doing?" my friend shouted as I grabbed a pint glass and pulled on a beer tap.

"I'm pouring a drink," I laughed.

Soon, my friends followed suit, pouring themselves a drink while leaving a generous tip for the brawling bartenders outside. When life hands you lemons, pour yourself a beer.

THE THREE MARIAS

My brother, Fredo, spent little time on patrol before opting for an administrative position inside the precinct. His fifteen minutes of fame came as a rookie cop when he and his partner raced a breathless infant to the hospital, saving the child's life. The heroic event landed Fredo and his partner on the front page of *The Daily News*.

"Hey, jerkoff, did you see your brother in the newspaper?" my father laughed.

My father knew how to push my buttons, comparing me to my younger brother. I took my police career seriously. Fredo viewed the NYPD as a job with a paycheck and showed little interest in making arrests or his performance reviews. I ignored my father's attempt to pit me against my younger brother and told him to pound sand.

Less than a year later, my brother's partner was in the news again; this time, it was for taking a life. After a night of heavy drinking in Las Tres Marias (The Three Marias) bar, the Harlem cop fought with another patron when his gun came out. The drunken cop shot a customer in the arm before the bullet ricocheted and struck a woman in the head. When the story broke, I took a copy of the article to show my father.

"So? Your brother didn't shoot anybody," my father barked.

"Maybe your son should be more careful with the company he keeps," I replied.

My brother's ex-partner received an eight-year prison sentence for his recklessness. After the tragedy, bar patrons referred to the bar as Las Dos Marias.

My advice for young cops is to be just as careful of your surroundings off-duty as you are at work. Unfortunately, cops are expendable these days, and police departments no longer give second chances. When you're in a licensed premise, and someone gets loud or a fight breaks out, it's time to go home. Hanging around to watch the action will land you in hot water. You can get hurt physically or wind up a witness to something you shouldn't have been around in the first place. Avoid neighborhood dive bars where local tough guys are looking to make an example of someone. If you stop for a drink after work, go with a group of coworkers, and don't overindulge. A cop's actions will always be judged in the court of public opinion. Unfortunately, off-duty errors in judgment have ended many law enforcement careers.

CHAPTER 10

NYPD POTPOURRI

Unfortunately, my childhood fear of anesthesia is catching up with me. The older I get, the more doctor visits and medical procedures I have to endure. It's been almost ten years since my last visit to my gastroenterologist, and I knew what was coming.

"Vic, you're due for a colonoscopy," the doctor said.

I agreed to the medieval procedure, provided I could do it without anesthesia.

"You know it's a lot easier when the patient is asleep," the doctor cautioned.

"Easier for who?" I replied.

Nothing had changed since my last colonoscopy ten years earlier. From start to finish, it was twenty-four hours of living hell. Fasting for thirty hours would drive Tony Robbins to madness as your blood sugar level sinks like the *Titanic*. Drinking sixty-four ounces of laxatives in four hours overwhelms your stomach to the point where all hell breaks loose. On the day of the procedure, you're asked about living wills and told to strip to your birthday suit while a disinterested nurse runs an IV into your vein.

Eventually you find yourself in a brightly lit room surrounded by strangers in surgical scrubs. Before you know it, Roto-Rooter is working his way past your sigmoid colon. It was a painful twenty minutes of lying on my side while the talkative gastroenterologist explored my intestines.

"Everything's good," he said, pulling the tube out of my ass.

After the procedure, a nurse wheeled me into a small bay in the recovery room.

"I wasn't sedated. I want to go home," I said.

"I have to monitor your vital signs for a few minutes. Then you can be on your way," the nurse explained.

While making small talk, I mentioned that I was a retired New York City police detective.

"What's your tax number?" a weak voice asked through the shower curtain partition.

"Tax number?" I haven't heard that term in years.

A tax number is a six-digit number assigned to every member of the New York City Police Department. The numbers are in sequential order and handed out on the day you're hired. Only an active or retired member of the Department would only know what a tax number is.

"You were on the job?" I shouted back.

"What's your tax number?" he mumbled.

"Who is that?" I asked the nurse.

"Another patient. He's still groggy from the anesthesia," she explained.

"What's your tax number?" the dazed voice repeated.

I shouted my six-digit tax number through the curtain as the nurse removed the IV from my arm.

The semi-conscious voice replied: "Oh wow, you're an old timer."

Old timer? I'm in my mid-fifties. I joined the NYPD in 1987. Old timers were the guys who came on the job in the sixties with thick sideburns and porn mustaches. I'm not an old timer. I'm a retired middle-aged man.

"Where did you work?" I asked.

"The seven five and the eight three," he replied.

"A Brooklyn guy?" I asked.

For several minutes, my semiconscious friend and I reminisced about our NYPD careers through a plastic curtain.

"Do you guys know each other?" the recovery room nurse asked.

"Kinda," I replied.

It's safe to say you can't throw a rock in the Sunshine State without hitting a retired NYPD member.

SPIDER SENSE

Now retired sixteen years later, I take my observation skills for granted until I'm reminded that I'm wired differently.

"Vic, I'll never forget the time I met you and your partner in Manhattan," my friend said.

Years earlier, the native Floridian was visiting the Big Apple and invited my partner and me to lunch.

I was fuzzy on the details of the twenty-years-ago event, but my friend remembered it like it was yesterday.

"Do you remember the woman in a mink coat smoking a cigarette in front of the restaurant?" he asked.

"John, what are you talking about?" I replied.

My friend explained the well-dressed socialite was enjoying a cigarette several feet away from a homeless man when I made a prediction.

"Watch what happens when she's done with that cigarette. The homeless guy will grab it off the sidewalk and take a puff before it burns out," I said.

"Sure enough, the woman finishes the cigarette and tosses it to the ground when the homeless guy swoops in and takes a drag," my friend explained.

The decades-old event held little significance for me, but my friend was amazed all these years later by my ability to predict human behavior.

"How did you know the homeless guy would pick up the cigarette?" my friend asked.

I tried explaining to my civilian friend how cops are trained to observe and read body language, but he wasn't grasping it.

"Yeah, but how did you know?" he asked again.

"My spider sense was tingling," I replied.

SHERIFF GRADY JUDD

Writing a book doesn't guarantee anyone will read it. Self-published authors face the uphill battle of readers discovering their books. You have to market your book without the luxury of a major publishing house. I spend a third of my time convincing podcast hosts I can provide interesting content for their shows. If you want to sell books, you have to sell yourself. Podcasts are the perfect venue for authors to promote their books. If you can tell a story and people find you interesting, chances are they'll purchase your book. To accomplish this, I do up to ten interviews a week. There are plenty of podcasts looking for guests. Most podcast hosts are prepared and professional. Others are half-assed hobbyists who enjoy FaceTiming strangers.

One podcast was a game changer for me. I got lucky and got booked on Sean Sticks Larkin's podcast Cops & Cocktails. His producers instructed me to have a few drinks before the show. A few minutes into the interview, I swore like a sailor, sharing colorful stories from my NYPD career. After my episode aired on YouTube, my book sales went through the roof. Who knew a liquored-up Vic Ferrari dropping F-bombs would go viral?

Another time, I got suckered into a low-budget livestream from a dimly lit basement in Saskatchewan. Buffalo Bill's studio featured a variety of creepy taxidermy lurking in the background. The middle-aged outdoorsman asked bizarre questions while tending to a restless cat in his crotch. I found it difficult to concentrate as Blofeld stroked his kitty. Closer to home, I discovered a local radio show to promote my books.

After the interview, the program director offered me a job. It was an excellent opportunity to learn about broadcasting. A few months later, I was co-hosting the program. The low-budget radio show had a lineup of postmenopausal life coaches and snake oil salesmen pitching promises of eternal life. When the program director asked if there was someone I'd like to have on the show, I could only think of one name. Coming from a law enforcement background, I suggested Polk County Sheriff Grady Judd. For those of you living outside the Sunshine State, the outspoken law and order sheriff is known for his entertaining press conferences. Sheriff Judd is an elected official, but he's anything but a politician. Grady shoots from the hip and lets the chips fall where they may. His news conferences are legendary, often pointing out the inconvenient truth to an astonished press core.

When a deputy was murdered, a manhunt ensued until the fugitive was killed in a gun battle with Polk County sheriff's deputies. When asked why his deputies shot the suspect sixty-eight times, Grady replied, "That's all the bullets we had, or we would have shot him more."

During the 2020 riots, Sheriff Judd was asked about the possibility of civil unrest descending on his county. He replied, "If you value your life, you probably shouldn't do that in Polk County. Because the people of Polk County like guns, they have guns, and I encourage them to own guns, and they're going to be in their homes tonight with their guns loaded, and if you break into their homes to steal, to set fires, I highly recommend they blow you (looters) back out the house with their guns."

Sheriff Grady Judd would be a major upgrade to the previous guests we had as on the show.

"Do you think he would do an interview?" my co-host asked.

"We won't know until we ask," I replied.

We arranged a pre-interview at the Polk County sheriff's office a few days later.

On the morning of our interview, my co-host began planning her afternoon.

"We'll be done by ten?" she asked.

"Nah, more like noon," I replied.

"It won't take two hours for an interview."

"They are not going to let us breeze in there and knock on his door."

"What are you talking about?" my co-host asked.

"We're entering a police facility," I replied.

"So?" she said.

"Let me tell you how this is going to go. First, a couple of deputies will walk us through a magnetometer. Then, the director of public information will take us to his office for a little chat," I explained.

"I already spoke to the public information director. Why would he want to speak to me again?" she asked.

"Because he wants to be sure he's not sending a couple of clowns into his boss's office," I replied.

As predicted, we passed through a magnetometer before stopping by the director of the public information office, where he assessed our intentions over an assortment of pastries and coffee.

"Listen, we're huge fans of Sheriff Judd. We're not here to do a hit piece," I explained.

"Sheriff Judd takes all comers," the deputy replied.

"Is there anything off limits or we shouldn't ask?" I asked.

"You can ask anything you'd like. If Sheriff Judd doesn't want to talk about something, he'll be the first to tell you," the deputy replied.

After our coffee, the public information director led us into Sheriff Judd's office.

"Please make yourselves comfortable. Sheriff Judd will be here shortly," our guide explained before taking a seat behind my cohost and me.

He was making sure we were on the up and up and would sit through the interview.

Sheriff Judd entered the room a few minutes late, extending his hand with a friendly hello.

"You have a good man here," I said, pointing to his public information director.

"You know, after a few of those press conferences, I needed an agent to manage my appearances," Sheriff Judd laughed.

"I'm sure you get many requests," I said.

"It's not only that. Some mornings, I'd come into work, and there'd be a line of people hanging around the lobby waiting to take a picture with me," he said.

"I guess that makes it difficult to get any work done," I laughed.

"Public relations is part of the job. But when German tourists on their way to Walt Disney World stop by to meet the sheriff, I had to make some policy changes," Sheriff Judd explained.

We discussed a litany of police-related topics, including his rock star status among the rank-and-file members of the New York City Police Department. I explained to Sheriff Judd's surprise that my office would fall silent when he appeared on television. "Hey, that sheriff from Florida is on TV. Turn up the volume," was shouted so we wouldn't miss one of his classic quotes.

Sheriff Judd was a gracious host who took the time out of his busy schedule to sit down with two nobodies from a low-budget radio program. I've met many famous people during my time with the New York City Police Department. And I've never met anyone as authentic as Grady Judd. I doubt he would be interested, but I hope Sheriff Judd runs for higher office because this country needs more men like him.

CHAPTER 11

LAST OF THE MOHICANS

Now retired sixteen years, I don't get out of bed before ten. Early to bed, early to rise is a novel concept, but I can't do it. I like to sleep in and won't talk to anyone before my second cup of coffee. Everyone knows this except my six-year-old Irish Wolfhound. He doesn't care about morning fog or circadian rhythm. His bowels run like a German train schedule and don't tolerate delays. After several minutes of his badgering, I grab his leash and a plastic bag for our morning walk. My hound and I are a traveling comedy team providing entertainment for our subdivision.

Captain Crap would drop anchor anywhere, including the neighbor's lawn, as they dined on the front patio. Mortified, I bent down to scoop up the poop when Caligula circled behind and shoved his nose up my ass. Corn-hole Alfresco is one of the many hidden dangers to owning an Irish Wolfhound. Walking a hundred-and-twenty-pound dog is like transporting a prisoner. You must be alert at all times, or bad things will happen. If you're not, the neighbor's crotch is fair game, and piss is running down your leg.

Last summer, during our morning walk, my phone rang. *Who the hell is calling me now?* Rarely would I answer my phone before noon, but it was my buddy Mark from the police academy, so I made an exception.

Mark and I met on our first day at the police academy and have remained friends since. I got a kick out of the former Staten

Island ambulance mechanic because he could tell the difference between perception and reality.

Mark's father, a former cop, educated his son on what to expect working for the New York City Police Department.

The police academy was six months of head games designed to keep you on your toes. While I sweated bullets over pop quizzes, Mark didn't seem to have a care in the world.

"Vic, would you lighten up? They're not going to shoot you," he'd laugh when I'd worry over something trivial.

The police academy is like middle school. You're only there a short time with kids you'll never see again after graduation. With seventy-seven NYPD precincts spread across New York City's five boroughs, it was safe to say most of us would lose contact after the police academy. Surprisingly, I did run into several of my fellow recruits over the years.

"Long time, no see. Where are you working now?" was the extent of the conversation. It's not like I wasn't glad to see my former classmates. But we had grown up and gone our separate ways. Most of the time, the only thing we had in common was the six months we spent together in the police academy. Mark was the exception to the rule. Over the last thirty-five years, we'd kept in touch despite living on opposite ends of the city.

When I retired from the NYPD, I contacted Mark and encouraged him to do the same.

"Vic, I have a wife and three kids. It will be awhile before I can retire," he groaned.

Untethered, I could sail off into the sunset after a twenty-year career. Mark had responsibilities. He had to hang around for a while.

Over the years, when I'd bring up retirement with my police academy buddy, he'd laugh and repeat the mantra, "Vic, I have a wife and three kids."

Three and a half decades later, Mark changed his tune.

"Vic, you won't believe this. I put in my papers yesterday," he said.

"You retired?"

"I sure did."

"Congratulations, it's about time."

"Yeah, thirty-five years was more than enough."

"Time flies," I reflected.

"Did you know I'm the last police recruit from our company to retire?" Mark said.

"Really?"

"Yup, I'm the last of the Mohicans," Mark proclaimed.

"How do you know?"

"Remember those index cards we had to fill out in the police academy?"

"I do. We had to list our contact information and staple a passport photo to the top of the card?" I said.

"That's them," Mark laughed.

"What about them?"

"I have them."

"What are you talking about?" I asked.

"A few years ago, I ran into one of our police academy instructors, and he gave me our company's contact information cards."

"Could you email that to me? I'd love to find out what happened to these people," I asked.

Mark agreed it would be interesting to see the different paths our police academy classmates took over the years and promised to send them over.

After catching up with my fellow retiree, it was time to go home and do a little digging. I went into a closet and pulled out a shoebox filled with photos from my NYPD career. After thumbing through the stack, I found what I was looking for. A photograph of my police academy company.

Gazing at the decades-old photo, I was surprised at how much I had changed. I had filled out, adding ten pounds to my once skinny frame. What killed me was my jet-black hair was replaced by fifty shades of gray.

I began wondering where all the time went. After graduating high school, I had a string of dead-end jobs before becoming a police recruit. For me, the police academy was a culture shock.

I was expected to wear a uniform, be on time, and keep my mouth shut. During the six months of training, I was overwhelmed with countless rules and regulations while police academy instructors critiqued my every move. It was a lot to digest for a young man who often questioned authority.

As much as I despised the police academy, my classmates made the experience bearable. Without their encouragement and support, I would have dropped out of the police academy. Except for Mark, I hadn't spoken with any of my former classmates in years.

Mark emailed me a file containing twenty-seven scanned index cards the following day. I had mixed emotions researching my former coworkers' NYPD careers. I didn't know what to expect or how it would affect me.

It would take weeks of research before I sorted out this decades-old mystery.

Some names brought back fond memories. Others I struggled to remember. Most of my former police academy classmates had successful careers. Some fell on hard times. A few met with tragic ends. It's not what I had expected, but a lot can happen in thirty-five years.

A few weeks after graduating from the police academy, one classmate suffered a heart attack while pursuing a robbery suspect in the Bronx, ending his NYPD career. Two resigned a few months later to pursue careers in the private sector. One guy opened a restaurant. The other became a psychologist. Four colleagues left the NYPD for higher-paying jobs with the Nassau and Suffolk County police departments. Ten traded in their white police shields, rising through the department ranks. Four were promoted to detective, three became sergeants, two made it to lieutenant, and one to the rank of deputy inspector. A pair was fired for inappropriate behavior. One pointed his gun at a motorist during a traffic dispute. The other got liquored up and fired his gun on a crowded Manhattan street.

Sadly, five of my former police academy classmates had passed from a variety of misfortunes, ranging from a drug overdose, multiple sclerosis, AIDS, COVID-19, and a motorcycle accident.

After compiling the data, I called Mark to share what I had learned.

"Wow, Vic, you tracked down almost everyone from our police academy company."

"I would have made a hell of a detective," I joked.

"You know, I'd love to find out what happened to that crazy son of a bitch, Billy."

"The Mad Farter?" I asked.

The former boiler room stockbroker was a one-man crime wave who somehow had made his way into the police academy. The Michael Dukakis look-alike never let the rules get in the way of a good time. During our six months of training, the Wall Street grifter carpet-bombed classrooms with an endless supply of methane. His ability to fart on command earned him the nickname the Mad Farter.

He was famous for unleashing thunderous farts in physical training class, causing the crowded gymnasium to break into laughter. As funny as it was, the gym instructors weren't laughing. They'd lose their minds, demanding to know who broke wind during synchronized push-ups.

No one gave up the source of the well-timed farts, so our company often had to endure standing at attention on the roof of the police academy after class. The Mad Farter possessed a genius IQ but lacked the moral compass to work in law enforcement. The Chilean con man was dangerous and unpredictable, once challenging me to a gunfight in the third-floor bathroom. There is so much more to this lunatic story that I encourage you to read my book *The NYPD's Flying Circus: Cops, Crime & Chaos* for a better perspective.

"Who the hell knows," I replied.

"He was an enigma," Mark laughed.

"Just saying his name makes the hair on my neck stand up," I admitted.

"I know what you're saying, but I'd still love to know what happened to him," Mark pondered.

"Did you not forget he's crazy?"

"Morbid curiosity," Mark reasoned.

"Let's say you find him. Once you open that door, you won't be able to close it," I warned.

"You're right, Vic. Let sleeping dogs lie. Nothing good would come from lifting that rock."

RETURN OF THE FARTER

I screen my calls because I'm besieged by telemarketers selling everything from health insurance to hemorrhoid cream.

If I don't recognize the number, it goes to voicemail. A few weeks after speaking to Mark, I received several creepy voicemails from a South Florida area code. "Ferrari, we need to talk. Ha, ha, ha," he laughed and hung up.

"Who do I know in Miami?" I thought, trying to recognize the sinister voice. After several days of tormenting voice messages, I took the joker's call.

"Yeah?" I answered.

"Ferrari, long time, no see," the mocking voice laughed.

"Who the fuck is this?"

"Come on, Ferrari, is that how you talk to an old friend?" he snickered.

"Listen, pal. I'm not playing this game. Tell me what you want, or I'm blocking you."

"Jesus, Ferrari, I remember when you had a sense of humor."

"When was that?"

"The police academy," he replied.

Oh shit. Why did I take this call? I had stepped on a Bouncing Betty, and there was no place to run. Thirty-five years after graduating from the police academy, the missing puzzle piece had fallen into place. Crazy Billy, AKA the Mad Farter, was back.

Before this impromptu call, I would have bet Billy was dead or in jail because of his nefarious lifestyle. Now the question begged to be asked: How the fuck did this lunatic get a hold of my number?

"Hey, Billy, how are you?" I asked.

"I'm doing great. Living the dream in South Beach."

Some things never change. Billy was a slippery salesman who could sell ice to an Eskimo. This call wasn't to see how I was doing after all these years. Billy had something up his sleeve, and I had to keep him at arm's length.

"What have you been up to, Vic?"

"I retired from the job and moved to Florida."

"That's great! Are you keeping busy?" the Mad Farter asked.

"I am. I've written a series of books about the NYPD."

"That's great! Am I in any of them?"

Talk about an ego. I haven't heard from this guy in thirty-five years, and he's curious if he's made it into one of my books. The reality is I wrote an entire chapter about him (including burning his car for the insurance money), but I wasn't about to share that with him.

"Sorry, Billy, you didn't make the cut."

"Are you sure about that?" he asked.

Did he know? Or was this a bluff to see what he could squeeze out of me? Billy loved head games. He had Hannibal Lecter's ability to size a person up before going in for the kill. After several seconds of silence, I came to my senses. Billy didn't strike me as a voracious reader, so chances were he never heard of my books.

"Yeah, I'm sure. Maybe I'll put you in my next one," I laughed.

I revealed little about my personal life during the uncomfortable conversation. It was bad enough this snake oil salesman had somehow got my phone number. I didn't want him showing up on my doorstep. As far as what Billy was up to for the last thirty-five years, he wasn't saying much. The past was irrelevant. He was now selling solar panels in South Florida.

According to the Mad Farter, business was booming, and he wanted to bring me on as an investor with his burgeoning company.

I kept quiet while Billy Madoff laid out his latest Ponzi scheme. After listening to his pitch, I explained I'd consider the generous offer while trying to get him off the phone as quickly as possible.

"Ferrari, keep in touch," Billy instructed.

"Absolutely," I replied before hanging up.

The fuck I am. I'm blocking this crazy son of a bitch as soon as I can reach my thirteen-year-old nephew.

But before I called my IT guy, I had to share the news with Mark.

"You will not believe who called me."

"Who?" Mark asked.

"The Mad Farter."

"Wow. We were just talking about him. What's he up to?"

"Funny you should ask. Billy wants me to invest in some scam he's running in South Florida."

"Some things never change," Mark said.

"He was asking about you. I hope you don't mind that I gave him your phone number."

"Vic, don't fuck around. I still have nightmares from carpooling with that maniac."

"Don't worry, your name never came up," I laughed.

"Oh, thank God. I'm guessing you blocked him in your phone?"

"As soon as I can get a hold of my nephew."

"Your nephew?" Mark asked.

"Yeah, I don't know how to do that," I said.

Thirty-five years later, Billy was still hustling acquaintances. Calling an old lead, Billy figured he could relieve me of some cash while reminiscing about our days at the police academy. Unfortunately for Billy, school was out. I knew his act and wouldn't allow him to contact me again. After I got off the phone with Mark, I called my teenage protégé to block Billy from my iPhone.

"Uncle Vic, blocking a phone number is so easy. Let me walk you through it," my nephew laughed.

My thirteen-year-old nephew loves tormenting me. He's been pushing my buttons since the day he could crawl and never misses an opportunity to bust my balls.

Like when he told me he wanted to become a fireman instead of a police officer. I don't know where I've gone wrong with this kid. Maybe he spends too much time with his sarcastic uncle.

"Armand, I'm not doing this over the phone. Just be home after school tomorrow," I pleaded.

"Let me look at my schedule," he giggled.

Schedule? It wasn't too long ago this kid was crapping into a diaper.

"Listen, smart ass, if you want a laptop for Christmas, you better clear your schedule."

"Uncle Vic, stop by tomorrow afternoon, and I'll take care of it for you."

Problem solved. Now, all I had to do was maintain radio silence for the next twenty-four hours, and I'd never have to deal with the Mad Farter again. That was the plan until the following morning when I received Billy's rambling group text message.

"Some of you fucking clowns aren't meeting your goals," the message read.

The Mad Farter was cracking the whip. Channeling his inner *Glengarry Glen Ross*, he scolded his sales team for their low sales production.

"You pussies had better grow a pair of balls and start selling," the Mad Farter cautioned.

As bad as the bullying was, it was Billy's closing statement that reminded me how insane he was.

"And for those of you that don't meet your revenue expectations," the message read was followed with a photo of a giant turd floating in a toilet bowl.

It was obvious Billy's company needed a human resources department. Threatening to take a shit on your sales staff in a text message can open you to endless litigation. Billy's house of cards was about to come down, and I didn't want to be deposed in the upcoming lawsuit.

Later that day, I met with my nephew to block Billy from my life.

"Uncle Vic, who is this guy you want to block?"

"I was in the police academy with him many years ago."

"And?"

"He's crazy, and I don't want him calling me."

"How is he crazy?" my nephew pressed.

I gave him an earful about the Mad Farter. Stories of farting in classrooms, setting cars on fire, and shaving off an eyebrow resonated with my teenage nephew.

"Is it all right if I have his number?" he asked.

"Be careful what you wish for, Armand," I replied, snatching the phone out of his hand.

Billy was out of my life, and there was no looking back. Sometimes, you're better off not knowing what happened to someone from your past. If you haven't spoken to them after thirty-five years, chances are there's a reason for it.

CLOSING THOUGHTS

When you write a book, you get asked lots of questions. The question I'm asked most is what got me into writing. The simple answer is that I had to find something to do with my time after my NYPD career. I realized nothing could replace the excitement and adrenaline rush of police work. So I did the next best thing: write books about my former career. I knew I could write because my lieutenant would often kick back my reports with a smile.

"Vic, this is funny," Chumley laughed, waving a DD5 form in his hand.

"Thanks, Lieutenant."

"It's a shame. But you have to redo this five," he would say, handing me back the lengthy form.

"Why?" I asked.

"Vic, just because I think it's funny doesn't mean the powers that be at Police Plaza will."

Seven books later, I believe I've found my niche. My biggest regret is that my father never saw his son become an author. He would often tease that I would find my purpose in life one day.

"You know, Vic, one day you're going to be good at something," he'd laugh.

My father was a provocateur and loved to stir the pot. Despite knowing this, I'd always take the bait.

"Dad, what are you talking about? I'm a detective in the New York City Police Department."

"Not that crap. I'm talking about something important," my father replied, digging his fingers into a bowl of mixed nuts.

"Jesus, Dad, use the serving spoon."

"Listen, Miss Manners, they're my peanuts," he snapped.

It was dangerous to enter my father's vortex. He could have you spinning your wheels for days with innuendos and backhanded compliments.

"Dad, use the serving spoon. It's right here," I said, pointing with my finger.

"See, that's what I'm talking about. Maybe you can become a party planner?"

"Dad, I'm quite happy with my career."

"You'll figure it out one day," he said, licking the salt off his fingers.

Sadly, my father passed away a few months after I retired from the NYPD. His death left lots of unanswered questions. How did he overcome dyslexia? After the birth of a healthy and well-adjusted son, why did my parents tempt fate and bring Fredo into this world? These are the questions that keep me up at night.

Another question I'm asked is whether I was afraid of getting killed during my NYPD career. The simple answer is no. I never thought about losing my life. Was I scared to lose my job or get brought up on department charges? You bet I was, and it weighed heavily on me.

Most cops fear getting in trouble more than losing their lives. I never wanted to jump out of a plane or ride a motorcycle because I find those activities dangerous. But if you told me to throw on my uniform and stand on a corner in the South Bronx, I'd do it without hesitation. Despite all the bullshit, I loved my job. Sometimes I couldn't believe I was getting paid to do it.

Lately, I'm asked what my brother Fredo thinks of his portrayal in my book *Confessions of a Catholic High School Graduate*. Believe it or not, he loved it and wants me to write a sequel. Believe me when I tell you, you can't insult the guy. I'm also asked if I miss my former NYPD career. Now retired over sixteen years, I miss the clowns, not the circus.

My next book is going to be funny. It details several wild summers I spent at the Jersey Shore. *Sun, Sand, and Speedos* provide a Norman Rockwell backdrop to a poorly installed air conditioner falling three stories out of a Victorian window. There's no Snooki or Pauly, but plenty of embarrassing situations.

If you want to hear more NYPD stories, I encourage you to listen to my podcast: **NYPD Through the Looking Glass.** The show features a weekly lineup of retired NYPD members who share experiences. Recently, a retired transit cop told a story about a guy so hellbent on committing suicide that he threw himself on the subway tracks where he broke his arm. Annoyed, the sad sack dragged himself across the tracks and grabbed the third rail. Instead of getting electrocuted, the six hundred volts of electricity blew his arm off his body. If you are wondering, yes, he survived. My podcast is available on Buzzsprout, Apple Podcasts, Spotify, Google Podcasts, iHeartRadio, Castro, YouTube, and other podcast directories.

As always, I want to thank all of you for spending your hard-earned money on my books. I know it wasn't an easy decision, given today's economy.

All reviews, good, bad, and indifferent, have helped me become a better writer. I read every review and welcome your feedback. If you enjoyed *NYPD Laughing in the Line of Duty* be sure to check out my other books.

Dickheads & Debauchery
and Other Ingenious Ways to Die.

NYPD Through the Looking Glass Stories from Inside America's Largest Police Department

The NYPD's Flying Circus Cops Crime & Chaos

Grand Theft Auto: The NYPD's Auto Crime Division

NYPD Law & Disorder

Confessions of a Catholic High School Graduate

You can preview all my books for free on Amazon by clicking the hyperlink below.
https://www.amazon.com/stores/Vic-Ferrari/author/B01IIQXLBC?

All persons mentioned in this book are fictitious. Locations, time periods, precincts, ranks, individuals, names, events, and dates have been changed, conjured, invented, exaggerated, or blended and are fictitious embellishments made to paint a lighthearted portrait of the New York City Police Department.

Thank you again, and please be safe in these uncertain times.

Hopefully, I'll see you all soon.

WHAT'S IN A NAME?

What's in a name, you ask? Plenty. On December 3, 1978, a mob of three thousand people stormed the Sixty-Sixth Precinct in Brooklyn to protest the murder of a community member. The riot left sixty-two NYPD members injured, earning the precinct the nickname of Fort Surrender. Every NYPD precinct or specialized unit has a unique nickname. Each moniker provides provenance to the command's reputation. Some nicknames are more flattering than others, but I'm sure you get the general idea.

One Police Plaza - Paper Pushing Plaza, Fourteen Floors of Whores

City Wide Traffic Task Force - The Island of Misfit Toys

Housing Police - Unavailable

Highway 2- The Gulag

Internal Affairs – Rat patrol, The Dark side

Midtown South - Midtown Soft

Outdoor Range - M*A*S*H, Prison chow line

Queens Task Force - Queens Marines

Tactical Patrol Force - Tasmanian Police Force, Those Poor Fucks

Transit - Steel Dust Ballroom

Street Crime Unit - We Own the Night

Scuba Unit - Bobbing for Bodies

Vice- Pimps & Hos, The Pussy Posse, No More Bets

First - Fighting First, It's fun in the one, If you're looking for crime, we have none

Fifth Shanghai Sally

Sixth - Raiders of the Lost Ark

Ninth - The Fighting Ninth, The Shit House

ABOUT THE AUTHOR

Vic Ferrari is a retired NYC detective who leads a fascinating life. Vic's written seven books, met four Academy Award winners, and had lunch with Billy Joel's trumpet player. When Vic's not tending to his needy Irish Wolfhound, he can be heard on the syndicated radio program Sterling on Sunday. For more insight and amazing stories about the New York City Police Department, check out Vic's NYPD Through the Looking Glass podcast.

Follow Vic on Twitter and Instagram @Vicferrari50.